Moshe A. Milevsky
Associate Professor of Finance,
Schulich School of Business, York University
Executive Director of the IFID Centre, Toronto

Life Annuities: An Optimal Product for Retirement Income

RESEARCH FOUNDATION
OF CFA INSTITUTE

Statement of Purpose

The Research Foundation of CFA Institute is a not-for-profit organization established to promote the development and dissemination of relevant research for investment practitioners worldwide.

The Research Foundation of CFA Institute and the Research Foundation logo are trademarks owned by The Research Foundation of CFA Institute. CFA®, Chartered Financial Analyst®, AIMR-PPS®, and GIPS® are just a few of the trademarks owned by CFA Institute. To view a list of CFA Institute trademarks and the Guide for the Use of CFA Institute Marks, please visit our website at www.cfainstitute.org.

© 2013 The Research Foundation of CFA Institute

ISBN 978-1-934667-56-9

17 May 2013

Editorial Staff

Elizabeth Collins
Book Editor

Abby Farson Pratt
Assistant Editor

Mike Dean
Publishing Technology Specialist

Cindy Maisannes
Manager, Publications Production

Christina Hampton
Publishing Technology Specialist

Randy Carila
Publishing Technology Specialist

Biography

Moshe A. Milevsky is an associate professor of finance at the Schulich School of Business and a member of the graduate faculty in the Department of Mathematics and Statistics at York University in Toronto, where he is also the executive director of the not-for-profit Individual Finance and Insurance Decisions (IFID) Centre. He has published 10 books and more than 60 peer-reviewed articles in such journals as *Insurance: Mathematics and Economics*, *Financial Analysts Journal*, *Journal of Risk and Insurance*, *Journal of Banking and Finance*, *Journal of Financial and Quantitative Analysis*, *Mathematical Finance*, *Journal of Pension Economics and Finance*, and *Journal of Portfolio Management*. In 2006, together with Roger G. Ibbotson, Peng Chen, CFA, and Kevin X. Zhu, Professor Milevsky was awarded a Graham and Dodd Scroll Award for their *Financial Analysts Journal* article on life-cycle financial planning, "Human Capital, Asset Allocation, and Life Insurance." In 2003, he was granted two national (Canada) magazine awards for his popular writing on personal finance. Professor Milevsky is a 2002 fellow of the Fields Institute for Research in Mathematical Sciences and has delivered more than 1,000 seminars and keynote presentations around the world on retirement income planning. He holds an MA from the Department of Mathematics and Statistics and a PhD in finance from the Schulich School of Business, both at York University in Toronto.

Contents

Foreword... vii

Preface... ix

Acknowledgments... xi

1. Institutional Details 1

    Q1. What Is a Life Annuity, and What Flavors Do They
Come In? 1

    Q2. How Long Have Life Annuities Been Available, and
Who Invented Them?.. 4

    Q3. How Are Life Annuities Related to Defined Benefit
Retirement Pensions?.. 6

    Q4. The Term Structure of Longevity-Contingent Claims:
What Do the Claims Yield?.. 10

    Q5. Historical Data: How Have Life Annuity Yields
Changed over Time?.. 13

    Q6. How Is Life Annuity Income Taxed, and Is It
Economically Neutral?... 16

    Q7. Who Sells Life Annuities (in North America), and How
Are They Regulated?.. 19

    Q8. What Does the Insurance Company Do with the
Premiums?.. 22

    Q9. Credit Risk: What Happens If the Company Goes
Bankrupt?... 24

    Q10. Do the Credit Ratings of the Insurance Company
Affect Payouts? 27

    Q11. A First Look at Methuselah Risk: What If Annuitants
Lived for 969 Years?.. 30

    Q12. Are Life Annuities Popular, and What Is the Size of
the U.S. Market?.. 33

    Q13. Is a Variable Annuity with a Guaranteed Lifetime
Withdrawal Benefit a Substitute for a Life Annuity? 35

2. Ten Formulas to Know 39

    Q14. What Is a Biological Mortality Rate, and How Is It
Measured?.. 39

    Q15. How Are Mortality Rates Converted into Survival
Probabilities? 41

    Q16. What Is the Benjamin Gompertz Law of Mortality?......... 45

    Q17. Valuation: What Is the Gompertz Annuity Pricing Model? 49

    Q18. What Are the Duration and Interest Rate Sensitivity
of a Life Annuity? 52

    Q19. What Is the Money's Worth Ratio of a Life Annuity? 54

Q20. Can You Afford to Wait? Introducing the Implied
    Longevity Yield... 57
Q21. What Is the Lifetime Ruin Probability from
    Self-Annuitizing?... 59
Q22. How Does a Variable Immediate Annuity Work?............. 62
Q23. What Is the Difference between a Tontine and a Life
    Annuity?... 65
3. The Scholarly Literature 69
The Life-Cycle Model and Life Annuities................................ 70
Actuarial Pricing, Valuation, and Reserving............................ 79
Optimal Product Allocation and Timing................................. 83
Defining and Solving the Annuity Puzzle................................ 94
The Money's Worth Ratio around the World............................ 104
Other Institutional and Policy Literature................................ 109
4. Conclusions and Final Thoughts 112
Final Takeaways of the Discussions 112
Imagining the Life Annuity of 2020 116
Bibliography 119

CE Qualified Activity ✺ **CFA Institute**   This publication qualifies for 5 CE credits under the guidelines of the CFA Institute Continuing Education Program.

Foreword

Of all the hurdles that individual investors face in saving for retirement, perhaps the most challenging is the need to avoid running out of money before they die. The technology that solves this problem—the life annuity—has existed for centuries and, amazingly, predates ordinary stocks and bonds. A life annuity is a contract in which an insurance company or other financial intermediary, having received the investor's capital, pays him or her a fixed income (which may or may not be adjusted for inflation) for the rest of the investor's life.

Could there be a more perfect marriage of need and ability, of demand and supply? Yet, few people actually invest in life annuities; the only guaranteed income they typically receive is the mandatory government-provided annuity known in the United States as Social Security. Instead, investors widely believe that life annuities are a "rip-off" sold by unscrupulous insurance companies to unsophisticated victims and refuse to consider them. Investors prefer to manage the savings decumulation (opposite of accumulation) process themselves. To do so, many use such heuristics as the 4% withdrawal rule, which is guaranteed to fail in some small, but significant, percentage of scenarios.

To help investors understand life annuities as an invaluable tool for creating retirement income that cannot be outlived, Professor Moshe Milevsky of York University in Toronto has produced a book that is delightfully entertaining and richly informative. He seems to have forgotten the rule that technically detailed material must be a tough read.

Longtime readers of Research Foundation books will remember Milevsky from a 2007 book he co-authored on the subject of how to achieve lifetime financial security.[1] In that work, the authors offered lifetime financial advice that included life annuities as an important element in one's tool kit. Here, Milevsky focuses on this particular financial instrument. He recounts the long history of life annuities (they existed in 1700 BCE and were popular, much later, among Roman soldiers) and delves into the details of how insurers today use modern statistical analysis to calculate the fair price of a life annuity.

Why Are Life Annuities Unpopular?

One of the obstacles to the use of annuities as a retirement tool may be the perception that annuitization is an all-or-nothing decision: You either annuitize your wealth—exchange it for a guaranteed lifetime income—or you manage decumulation yourself. Most people shy away from exchanging all

---

[1]Roger G. Ibbotson, Moshe A. Milevsky, Peng Chen, and Kevin X. Zhu, *Lifetime Financial Advice: Human Capital, Asset Allocation, and Insurance* (Charlottesville, VA: Research Foundation of CFA Institute, 2007).

their money (wealth or capital) for an income stream. The psychology goes something like this: Almost everyone has been without money at some point. Having escaped that predicament by accumulating a nest egg, they find parting with it just too difficult, no matter what the promised reward.

Moreover, the exchange of assets for income is not made easier by the large element of uncertainty surrounding whether one will live to receive the income. Even if the creditworthiness of the insurer or annuity issuer is perfect, the income stream continues only as long as the annuitant is alive. Thus, one might exchange one's life savings for an income stream that lasts only a year—or a month. Of course, if the deal is priced fairly, this outcome is balanced by the possibility of living to collect 40 or more years of payments when the annuity issuer is only expecting to pay out for 20 years. If the investor does in fact live a long time, his or her ability to collect annuity income is very important because going back to work becomes a less practical strategy with each passing year and is really quite unlikely at, say, age 105.

Making Retirement Assets Last a Lifetime

A more optimal solution, then, might be to buy a life annuity with some of one's wealth and hold the rest of it directly. In a recent *Financial Analysts Journal* article, the authors propose a retirement structure in which the investor saves enough to live from age 65 to 85 by using a self-managed strategy and also purchases a *deferred* life annuity in which the income does not begin until age 85 to provide for those older years. [2]

This structure is attractive partly because the deferred annuity is inexpensive. It's a bargain because the annuity is priced on the expectation that many annuitants will not live to age 85 and many more will live to collect for only a few years, so the issuer is on the hook for few payments. Annuitants who live to a very old age will profit tremendously at the expense of everyone else in the risk pool. At the same time, the annuitant keeps and manages most of his or her capital during the critical early years of retirement, when the individual has more opportunity for leisure-related spending and more options to earn money.

Milevsky presents the case for and against annuities structured with a variety of terms, conditions, bells, and whistles. And he presents the material with humor and clarity. The Research Foundation of CFA Institute is exceptionally pleased to present Milevsky's book. I cannot imagine a reader who will not be captivated by this tale.

Laurence B. Siegel
Gary P. Brinson Director of Research
Research Foundation of CFA Institute

---

[2]Stephen C. Sexauer, Michael W. Peskin, and Daniel P. Cassidy, "Making Retirement Income Last a Lifetime," *Financial Analysts Journal*, vol. 68, no. 1 (January/February 2012):74–87.

Preface

In a *Wall Street Journal* article published 18 April 2009, two veteran reporters, Anne Tergesen and Leslie Scism, wrote:

> For years, many retirees were content to act as their own pension managers, a complex task that involves making a nest egg last a lifetime. Now, reeling from the stock-market meltdown, many are calling it quits and buying annuities to do the job for them. In recent months, sales of plain-vanilla immediate annuities—essentially insurance contracts that convert a lump-sum payment into lifelong payouts—have hit an all-time high. (p. C1)

They then went on to state:

> While many investors have a general idea of what an annuity is, few understand the strategies available for making these products a part of their holdings. You have to figure out how much to buy, whether to put your money to work immediately or gradually, and how to invest what remains. (p. C1)

With these concerns in mind—and motivated by the practical aspects of the retirement challenge—I provide here an overview of the body of research on life annuities, longevity insurance, and the role of these investments in the "optimal" retirement portfolio. I start in Chapter 1 with a basic overview of the main institutional aspects, discuss more advanced and somewhat technical valuation issues in Chapter 2, and conclude in Chapter 3 with a comprehensive and self-contained review of the scholarly financial and economic literature on life annuities. Each of these three main chapters should be of interest to a distinct, but hopefully overlapping, group of readers.

The data, examples, and institutional features in this book are primarily U.S. based, and "dollars" are U.S. dollars unless otherwise noted.[3] Given my dual citizenship and current academic base at York University in Toronto, I contrast and compare elements with the Canadian market when possible without distracting from the main narrative. As far as I am concerned, this book is about life annuities in a North American context.

To make this potentially dry topic readable and accessible, the first two chapters are structured in a question-and-answer form, with answers that are each approximately 1,000 words in length. This format allows readers initially to skip directly to questions and issues that interest them and perhaps catch up on the rest at a later time. Because the fields of financial economics and

---

[3]I am a co-founder and CEO of the Quantitative Wealth Management Analytics (QWeMA) Group, which is a Toronto-based software consulting company serving the financial services industry. Note that some of the tables in this book use data generated by QWeMA Group employees. These instances are noted and acknowledged in the text.

actuarial insurance, which are logically closely related, have tended to develop separately, I focus on bringing *finance* practitioners and researchers up to speed on the mechanics, dynamics, and economics of life annuities, without requiring a degree in actuarial science or probability theory. So, my targeted audience includes PhDs, CFA charterholders, MBAs, Certified Financial Planners, Retirement Income Specialists, and other researchers, as well as practitioners in private wealth management and executives at firms that create and sell financial retirement products.

Given demographic trends, the decline in defined benefit pension coverage, and the widespread acknowledgment that current benefit projections for government pension programs are in jeopardy, financial advisers must prepare for their emerging role as personal pension plan managers. I believe—and most scholars in the field for the past 50 years have argued—that life annuities are a core component of the optimal retirement income portfolio. Hopefully, after reading this book, you will agree.

Acknowledgments

I would like to thank Walter (Bud) Haslett, CFA, executive director, and Laurence B. Siegel, research director, of the Research Foundation of CFA Institute for encouraging me to pursue this project and for providing ample and constructive feedback as this book was created. I thank the Research Foundation also for financial support. I would also like to thank my longtime research co-authors—specifically, Narat Charupat; Peng Chen, CFA; Huaxiong Huang; David Promislow; Chris Robinson; Thomas Salisbury; and Virginia Young—with whom I have been thinking, researching, and writing about retirement income and annuities for most of my academic life at York University in Canada. Thus, without implicating any of them in my mistakes, errors, and omissions, much of what follows can likely be traced to (long) conversations with members of a team I affectionately label my "Life Annuity Group of Seven."

In terms of the gritty details for this book, I thank Maxwell Serebryanny and Dajena Collaku (the IFID Centre), Simon Dabrowski (the Quantitative Wealth Management Analytics Group), Minjie Zhang (York University), Lowell Aronoff (Cannex), and finally Edna Milevsky (Family Inc.), all of whom provided comments on the manuscript and assisted with editing, sourcing, research, and compilation.

1. Institutional Details

Q1. What Is a Life Annuity, and What Flavors Do They Come In?

At the risk of sounding a bit eccentric, I will start by saying that a life annuity can be described as a *perpetual bond* (i.e., one that never matures and pays coupons forever) subject to a peculiar type of credit default risk, which I will describe shortly. In other words, a life annuity is a type of high-yield corporate bond. The yield on the life annuity bond is higher than the yield from a risk-free government bond because of the extra default risk assumed by the holder, which is a risk that grows over time. The life annuity bond is acquired with a lump-sum premium, and the coupons or income payments are paid monthly by the issuer (seller) to the holder (buyer). And like any interest-sensitive financial product, its price, or value, is inversely related to interest rates. When interest rates move higher, the annuity's value falls, and vice versa; in periods of (very) low interest rates, the value of a life annuity bond is (much) more expensive. In fact, just as with conventional bonds, you can purchase real (i.e., inflation-adjusted) life annuity bonds as well as nominal ones. The real ones are more expensive, but in exchange, the periodic coupon or income payments are adjusted for price inflation.

Of course, highlighting similarities is useful only up to a point, and the analogy of a high-yield corporate bond can take us only so far. Alas, in contrast to a conventional corporate bond, in which the defaulting party is the issuer or debtor, the party who causes payments to cease in the case of a life annuity is the holder of the bond. Moreover—and this point is the most critical and important distinction—the *triggering credit event is death*, not bankruptcy or insolvency. In other words, when the holder of the bond (the creditor or buyer) dies, the issuer (the debtor or seller) is no longer obligated to make coupon payments. Perhaps only an actuary would think of this characteristic as a default risk analogous to corporate bond default risk, but that is exactly what it is. In fact, many of the models used by financial analysts in the realm of credit risk analysis were actually first developed by actuaries for use in valuing life annuities.

Now, although there are many variations on this basic theme, I will continue to use the language of bonds—default triggers, debtors, and creditors—to help build the intuition for how a life annuity works. Nevertheless, from this point on, I will dispense with the word "bond" and use the term "life annuity" exclusively. I will also be careful to use the word "life" before "annuity," to distinguish a true life annuity from instruments and vehicles that use annuity in their (marketing) title but have nothing to do with bonds or income for the rest of your life. So, please do not confuse "XYZ insurance company–sold annuity" with "life annuity." It is the difference between using the term "fund" and the term "exchange-traded fund" (ETF). An ETF is obviously a fund, but calling something a fund does not mean that you can buy or sell it on an exchange or that its underlying holdings are stocks or bonds or anything else that you think of when hearing the designation "ETF."

Here is an example that should help explain how a life annuity works. Suppose in early September 2012, a 65-year-old male annuitant was quoted a figure of US$100,000 to purchase a life annuity paying $532 per month for the rest of the annuitant's life. He would receive $532 per month—which is $6,384 per year, and thus 6.4% of his $100,000 premium—as long as he remained alive. The payments would be fixed in nominal terms and would not be adjusted for inflation. And when he died, the payments would cease.

This price, which is usually quoted in terms of monthly payouts per $100,000, is the actual average of the top five vendors in the U.S. market in early September 2012.[4] Notice that the 6.4% yield is higher than the 3% yield available from 30-year U.S. Treasury bonds at the time—or from any perpetual bond, if such was available—(1) because of the mortality risk accepted by the annuitant and (2) because the 6.4% includes a return of capital over the annuitant's lifetime. That is, the annuitant takes the risk that he will die (early) and lose all future payments. This particular—and stark—manifestation could be described as a pure life annuity with no *period certain* (PC). Indeed, the annuitant (or his beneficiary) has no certainty of receiving any payments.

Another way to think of it is as a gamble: If the 65-year-old male annuitant lived for exactly 15.7 (100,000/6,384) more years, he would just barely get his original investment back. Every year he lived beyond age 80.7 would be pure "investment gravy"—of course, ignoring the time value of money or interest he could have earned on a T-bond instead. And if the annuitant died before age 80.7, he would "lose the bet," having paid $100,000 and received less, perhaps much less, in return. These breakeven winning and losing benchmarks are extremely rough estimates but can be excused at this early stage of our exploration.

Mechanics aside, you do not need a degree in behavioral finance to hypothesize that such a product—in which all is lost upon death—is not palatable to most investors. This is the likely reason that most life annuities are purchased with additional guarantees that provide assorted death benefits and/or that stipulate that payments must continue (to someone) in the event of death. Naturally, you do not need a degree in financial economics to appreciate why those enhanced annuities will be more expensive; that is, the monthly payments will be lower if all other things are equal. **Exhibit 1** provides a high-level summary of the many bells and whistles available when purchasing or investing in a life annuity.

---

[4]The source of this material is the QWeMA Group, Toronto, Canada.

Exhibit 1. Common Life Annuity Features

Terminology	Explanation	Popularity
Term certain	Nothing to do with life or longevity. Economically, it is a portfolio of zero-coupon bonds.	Only as a bond substitute.
0 PC	Payments cease at death, even if it occurs soon after the original purchase date. All is forfeited.	Rare form, viewed as too risky.
5-, 10-, 15-, or 20-year PC	Original payments guaranteed to continue to beneficiary up to a fixed number of years.	Common form purchased.
Joint and survivor at x%	Fraction of payment guaranteed to continue to a survivor (spouse) while that person is alive.	Common form purchased.
COLA at y% growth or CPI-linked, with maximum cap	Cost of living adjustment (COLA) at a fixed percentage yearly or linked to a consumer price index (CPI). More expensive; thus, less income.	Rarely purchased.
Refund annuity	In the event of early death, beneficiary gets refund of original purchase premium minus all payments received.	Increasingly popular option.
Advanced life delayed annuity (ALDA) or deferred income annuity (DIA)	Nonrefundable premium paid today, but income begins much later—assuming annuitant is still alive.	Small number of buyers but growing rapidly.

Exhibit 1 is not necessarily an exhaustive list of all the permutations available, and you can actually purchase a combination of the listed features. Think of it as a cafeteria menu. Thus, for example, a couple—say a 65-year-old male and a 62-year-old female—might spend $100,000 to purchase a life annuity with an 80% survivorship benefit and a 10-year PC. It might pay $400 per month while both annuitants were alive. If the primary holder—the male, in this case—died within 10 years of purchase, his spouse would continue to receive the $400 per month. Then, once the 10 years from the purchase date had passed, if she were still alive at age 72, she would continue to receive 80% of the $400, or $320, for the remainder of her life. Note that if both died during the 10-year PC, the heirs or beneficiaries would get $400 per month during the certainty period.

Notice the extra guarantees compared with the life-only version. The annuitants get only $400, compared with the previously described 65-year-old male who would be entitled to $532 per month. This difference represents the trade-off between risk and return and is at the heart of understanding life annuity pricing. In exchange for taking on mortality risk—that is, the risk that you might die "early" (and that your beneficiaries lose the original corpus[5]), you are entitled to higher payments while you are alive. The more guarantees, refunds, and options you add on to the life annuity, the more you water down the benefits of *longevity pooling*: The income that you receive from a life annuity—above and beyond your original principal and the interest it earns—is *other people's money*. It is a transfer, arranged by the insurance company through pooling of risk, from people who die while you remain alive. So, if you are not willing to forfeit your money to the pool when you die at some point by selecting long-dated guarantees, then all you are left with is an expensive bond product.

In the next section, I will step back and discuss the history of these products.

Q2. How Long Have Life Annuities Been Available, and Who Invented Them?

Nonspecialists are usually surprised to learn that life annuities existed and were widely used long before bonds ever traded. In fact, national governments used annuity-like instruments to finance deficits well before they borrowed by using the fixed-maturity bonds recognizable today. Life annuities have a long and illustrious history going back thousands of years. Their existence predates common stocks, saving bonds, and, certainly, mutual funds and ETFs. Yes, insurance companies—the only entities allowed to issue life annuities nowadays—have been around only since the middle of the 18th century, but churches, cities, and states issued life annuities (and *tontines*, which I will touch on later) long before then.

In fact, if you had to pinpoint the first life annuity ever purchased (or invented), it would probably be sometime around 1700 BCE, give or take a few centuries. According to research cited by Kopf (1927), archaeologists in Egypt

---

[5]Corpus is another way of saying original principal or investment.

uncovered evidence that a life annuity was purchased by a prince ruling the region of Sint in the Middle Kingdom (1100–1700 BCE). The annuitant's name was Prince Hepdefal, but we know little else about the annuity itself, in what units it was paid for, and whether it ended up being a good investment for him.

More recently—around the sixth century BCE—the Old Testament in 2 Kings, chapter 25, makes reference to the (life) annuity that was granted to Jehoiakim, king of Judah, on his release from prison, by the king of Babylon. By the second and third centuries CE, life annuities were quite popular in Rome, where mutual aid societies of the Roman legions granted them to soldiers who retired from military service at the age of 46. The life annuity's ubiquity is confirmed by the Roman jurist Ulpianus, who created a pricing matrix for life annuities based on the life expectancy of the annuitant. Although the prices themselves are crude from today's perspective, the document is popular with insurance historians and is known as the Table of Ulpian. See Kopf (1927) for more details.

Over the next 1,000 years, primarily monasteries and churches sold and dealt in life annuities. A well-known example (to insurance historians) is the annuity sold in 1308 CE by the abbot of St. Denis, not far from Paris, to the archbishop of Bremen. The archbishop paid 2,400 livres for the life annuity and, in exchange, was granted 400 livres per year, which is a yield of 16.66% for life and much more than you might expect today. Perhaps not surprisingly, 15 years after issuing the life annuity, the abbot, claiming that the amount was usurious, contested the payment to the archbishop.

Life annuities were viewed by many as a legitimate way of receiving interest without violating the laws and doctrines against usury. The rationale was that the mortality risk taken by both parties to the transaction made the instrument more of a gamble than a forbidden loan with interest. (Amusingly, interest was banned but gambling was acceptable.)

One of the earliest regions in which cities themselves (rather than religious organizations) issued life annuities was in the area of Flanders and Brabant (modern-day Belgium). Historians there have located detailed life annuity certificates (what we call "policies") dating back to the years 1228–1229.

By the 16th century, the granting, or sale, of annuities was done primarily by cities and governments to finance budget deficits. For example, in 1554, the Dutch Republic borrowed 100,000 guilders by selling life annuities—probably the first such sale by a government. The English did the same in 1693, during the reign of King William and Queen Mary, to finance a war against France.

Interestingly, most of the life annuities issued during this period did not offer age-based payouts. In other words, 30-, 60-, and presumably 90-year-olds were all offered the same rate, which today seems preposterous. In fact, scientists of that era predicted that this practice would lead to eventual problems. Edmond Halley, the famous British astronomer, wrote an influential

5

article in 1693 in which he formally priced a life annuity and showed how its payout *should* depend on age. Another century—and many more scandals and crises—would pass, however, before his ideas on properly pricing life annuities gained currency (an excellent early example of policymakers and governments ignoring the research of academics to the detriment of their citizens).

During the past 250 years or so, the sale of life annuities has been the exclusive purview of life insurance companies. And as they slowly took over the business, the insurance industry took better care to use scientific principles when pricing and quoting annuities. They created the field of actuarial science, hired actuaries, gathered mortality statistics, set reserves, and managed risk.

The first formal (incorporated) insurance company was the Equitable Life Assurance Society of London. Initially, it sold life insurance—making payments to widows and orphans—but it eventually graduated to selling life annuities. Sadly, life annuities almost caused the company's demise. In the year 2000, almost 240 years after receiving its royal charter, Equitable Life nearly went bankrupt because of guaranteed annuity promises it could not afford to keep. That story is told briefly in the later section on credit risk

Exhibit 2 provides a subjective bird's eye overview of the history of life annuities going back more than 3,500 years. Much more detailed and comprehensive reviews are available in Kopf (1927), Lewin (2003), and Poterba (2005), which are the underlying sources for most of the material in Exhibit 2.

Toward the early part of the 20th century, life annuities became intertwined with retirement pensions. In 1918, the industrialist Andrew Carnegie established in the United States the Teachers Insurance and Annuity Association (the TIAA part of what is today TIAA-CREF) to grant life annuities to retiring university professors and college teachers—many of whom lived in poverty once they stopped teaching.

By the end of the 20th century, retirement pensions and life annuities were often considered one and the same. The next section will discuss the economic similarities and regulatory differences between the two.

Q3. How Are Life Annuities Related to Defined Benefit Retirement Pensions?

Life annuities are often confused—justifiably—with defined benefit (DB) retirement pensions. Both instruments entitle the holder (annuitant or pensioner) to a guaranteed and predictable lifetime of income that cannot be outlived. The payments can be guaranteed for a fixed number of years, continue to a spouse and/or to beneficiaries, and or be adjusted for price inflation. To the novice (or theoretical economist), then, retirement pensions and life annuities

©2013 The Research Foundation of CFA Institute

Exhibit 2.   Important Milestones in the History of Life Annuities

Year	Event
1100–1700 BCE	Egyptian Prince Hepdefal, based in Sint in the period of the Middle Kingdom, acquires first recorded personal (life) annuity.
225 CE	Roman law jurist Domitius Ulpianus creates first pricing matrix for life annuities based on the life expectancy of the annuitant.
1554	The Dutch Republic (Holland) borrows 100,000 guilders by selling life annuities, which is the first time they are issued by a national government.
1671	Johan de Witt, the prime minister of Holland, derives a mathematical relationship between the price of a life annuity and term certain annuity, but unfortunately, he is subsequently lynched by a Dutch mob in the aftermath of the war with France.
1693	To go to war with France, the English government under King William and Queen Mary tries to borrow a million pounds by means of a tontine, a form of life annuity, that offers the same guaranteed dividend at all issue ages. One nominee actually lives to the age of 100. Also, the first asset pricing formula for a life annuity that proves age should affect payouts is developed by the English astronomer Edmond Halley. His pricing advice was ignored for centuries.
1720	Wide-spread annuity fraud problems are uncovered in England by relatives assuming the identity of dead annuitants and claiming their income. New regulations are imposed.
1762	The Equitable Life Assurance Society of London is formed. It is the first mutual insurance company to issue life insurance and then life annuities. It closed to new business in 2001 after massive losses on guaranteed annuities.
1918	Andrew Carnegie establishes Teachers Insurance and Annuity Association of America (TIAA) to grant (deferred) life annuities to retiring professors.
2012	More than $8 billion of individual life annuities are purchased every year from more than 25 major insurance companies in the United States and Canada.

should be viewed as the same thing. Yet, despite the similarities in terms of what they do and how they work, there are some key differences between them that are worth emphasizing.

First, an important aspect is that not all retirement pensions are actually taken as life annuities. Many retirees who are entitled to a life annuity opt instead to receive the payment in one large cash payout at the point of retirement. This choice is known as "cashing out" of a pension plan or taking a "lump-sum" payment. This option is not available with government pensions, such as Social Security (or the Canadian Pension Plan, CPP), but a number of employer-based pension plans do offer this choice. Taking the upfront cash when it is offered can be tempting.

Just as important is that not all retirement pension plans actually offer a life annuity option at retirement. In many cases, a DB plan is simply not part of the arrangement. In fact, defined contribution (DC) or money-purchase (MP) plans usually offer their participants or members only a lump-sum option when they leave or retire from service. If retirees want a life annuity, they must go to the retail market and buy it. They are on their own. In fact, some observers argue—and I am in this camp—that a retirement plan that offers its members a lump sum of money at retirement with no provision to exchange the lump sum for a guaranteed income should not be called a "pension plan" at all. It is a retirement savings plan or, perhaps, a retirement investment plan. If there is no life annuity at the end of the tunnel, then it is not truly a pension.

In my opinion, 401(k)s, 403(b)s, or IRAs (RRSPs or RPPs[6] in Canada) are not pension plans precisely because they do not provide guaranteed life annuities to their members at retirement. DB pension plans that promise a periodic stream of income at retirement (i.e., life annuities) are true pensions. (Some legal scholars disagree with me on this question, but almost all economists agree.)

Interestingly, a number of large DB (proper) pension plans that had promised their participants a lifetime annuity have recently offered their retirees (i.e., those receiving income already) an option to cash out and receive a lump sum. One of the more well-known cases involved General Motors (GM), which in the summer of 2012 offered more than 40,000 of its salaried retirees the option to stop their small monthly checks and receive, instead, one much larger check. Chapter 3 and the literature review discuss how people actually behave when given such choices.

In this case, moreover, for those retirees who opted to continue receiving their monthly pension checks (i.e., their life annuities), the obligation to make those payments was transferred to Prudential Finance, an insurance company. Either way, the plan was for GM to wash its hands of the relationship with retirees.

---

[6]Registered retirement savings plan and registered pension plan, respectively.

Although we do not know exactly how many ex-GM workers chose the lump sum over the life annuity, this offer was unprecedented. Note that it was given to people already in retirement—receiving their monthly income—as opposed to those about to retire. Such offers are a growing trend and show the close relationship between life annuities and retirement pensions.

Exhibit 3 displays some other aspects of the distinction between the two. For example, in the United States, a corporate pension plan, such as GM's plan, is regulated (i.e., monitored and policed) by the federal government. The Employee Retirement Income Security Act (ERISA) of 1974 is a federal law that sets minimum standards for pension plans in private industry. Although the U.S. Department of Labor (DOL) enforces ERISA, it does not require any employer to establish a pension plan. It only requires that those who do establish pension plans meet certain minimum standards. Think of the DOL as the watchdog.

Exhibit 3. Life Annuities vs. Retirement Pensions: Key Differences and Similarities

Key Feature	Life Annuity	Retirement Pension
Offered or sold by	Insurance company.	Employer or sponsor.
Purchase process	Pay lump-sum premium or via installments.	Based on work history, salary, and employer generosity.
Basis of payouts	Females must pay more for the same lifetime income because they live longer.	Based on years of service and salary. Companies cannot discriminate on the basis of gender or health.
How the money backing the income is invested	Insurance company invests conservatively in "general account" and is subject to extensive regulation.	Pension plan managers or sponsors must "manage [assets] prudently."
Regulation (in United States)	State regulators issue rules and guarantee funds.	U.S. DOL and ERISA legislation.
Protection (in United States)	National Organization of Life and Health Insurance Guaranty Associations (NOLHGA).	Pension Benefit Guaranty Corporation.
Value per dollar	Lower: pays "retail."	Higher: bought "wholesale."

In contrast, life annuities in the United States are sold by insurance companies and are regulated by individual states, not by the federal government. Regulatory policy is set by state legislatures, who then oversee state insurance departments, which, in turn, enforce state insurance laws. Although some insurance regulators are stricter than others—the New York office is notoriously vigilant—states tend to coordinate these activities among themselves via the National Association of Insurance Commissioners (NAIC), so it is not as though they all pull in completely different directions. (In Canada, the Office of the Superintendent of Financial Institutions Canada is the primary regulator and supervisor of federally regulated deposit-taking institutions, insurance companies, and federally regulated private pension plans.) All of these differences might sound somewhat legalistic and esoteric, but the federal versus state perspective does create a considerable difference between retirement pensions and life annuities. For example, if an insurance company goes bankrupt—a possibility worthy of its own section—the individual states oversee an insurance association–funded guarantee fund to help cover the losses. In contrast, if a pension plan runs into financial difficulty, the federal government's guarantee fund is the source of protection. (Neither of these kinds of funds will cover all the retiree's losses if they exceed certain limits.)

The regulation governing life annuities sold by insurance companies is far more stringent than the regulation governing retirement pensions, although they are similar economic instruments. Insurance companies must invest the money backing the annuity income conservatively and under regulation, but pension plan managers or sponsors are simply instructed to manage the assets "prudently," a vague order.

In summary, although an economist might consider a retirement pension to be the same as a life annuity, subtle legal and regulatory differences characterize the two. And if you ever have a choice between getting a lifetime of income from an insurance company or from a pension plan, one of the things you want to consider is who you want keeping an eye on your nest egg. If you believe that your state is competent at regulating financial institutions, then perhaps opt for the insurance company. If you prefer federal oversight, then perhaps the pension plan is the way to go.

Of course, more important than these legal technicalities is how much income you will actually receive, what the income level depends on, and how to get more. That is the topic of the next section.

Q4. The Term Structure of Longevity-Contingent Claims: What Do the Claims Yield?

Language is important, and when it comes to life annuities, the terminology can be confusing. The "cost" of a life annuity can be described in two ways. You can talk about the *price* of a life annuity or the *payout* from a life annuity.

The two are mirror images of each other and tend to be used interchangeably. Thus, for example, the price of obtaining a lifetime income of $1,000 per month might be a premium of $270,000 at age 65. In that case, the focus is on the cost of a given income stream. Or you can start with a given premium, say $100,000, and then talk about the payout being $435 per month. In both cases, the underlying economics of the transaction is the same. If you divide $270,000 by $12,000 (the annual income stream, 12 × $1,000), you get the same *annuity factor* of 14 in either case. Formally, the annuity factor is defined as the cost of $1 of income per year for the rest of your life. So, the cost of $1,000 or $10,000 or $100,000 per year is obtained by multiplying the annuity factor by the desired amount of income.

In most financial transactions, we customarily talk about the price per unit—for example, of an ounce of gold, a share of stock, or a carton of milk. But, when it comes to life annuities, the discussion tends to be in terms of the payout per $100,000 premium. This approach might seem odd at first; it is akin to discussing how much milk you might be able to get each day in exchange for a $100 one-time upfront payment. The convention to quote in terms of monthly income per $100,000 of premium paid is probably a historical artifact. Rest assured, if you want to buy an annuity, the insurance company will take any sum of money—as long as it is not too small—and will probably send you a check at the frequency you find most convenient. Rarely will you find volume discounts, although if you buy as part of a group—as in an employer pension plan—you will receive a better deal on the order of 10% or so. Also, you may have to pay a fixed policy fee—which is embedded in the quote—regardless of the size of the premium. So, there are some scale economies that reduce the fixed costs, but they don't really change the underlying mechanics of a life annuity.

Here is the key economic point: Whether you view the cost as price paid or payout received, the ratio between your premium (what you paid) and your annual income (what you get) will be the same and is called the "annuity yield."

Table 1 displays what these payouts were in August 2012 as a function of the buyer's age and gender and the guarantee period selected. This table shows what I call the "term structure" of longevity-contingent claims; some readers will recognize "term structure" from the literature and lingo of the bond market. Note that these prices—or, better stated, payouts—can change from week to week and often from day to day, just as bond prices do. So, do not expect to get these exact rates if you plan to purchase a life annuity any time soon. (I will later discuss where exactly these numbers come from.) Interest rate changes have a big impact on payouts and can happen anytime.

Table 1.   **Monthly Life Annuity Payouts Available per $100,000 Premium**

Age	0-Year PC	5-Year PC	10-Year PC	15-Year PC	20-Year PC
55	M = $431	M = $430	M = $427	M = $422	M = $414
	F = $416	F = $416	F = $414	F = $409	F = $403
60	M = $475	M = $473	M = $468	M = $459	M = $443
	F = $456	F = $455	F = $451	F = $443	F = $432
65	M = $532	M = $529	M = $519	M = $499	M = $470
	F = $507	F = $505	F = $497	F = $482	F = $461
70	M = $613	M = $606	M = $585	M = $544	M = $497
	F = $578	F = $574	F = $557	F = $527	F = $491
75	M = $729	M = $713	M = $664	M = $589	M = $516
	F = $686	F = $674	F = $635	F = $579	F = $513
80	M = $895	M = $865	M = $749	M = $623	M = $524
	F = $838	F = $809	F = $724	F = $617	F = $523

Note: M is male; F is female; PC is period certain.
Sources: QWeMA Group (August 2012). Based on data from Cannex Financial Exchanges. Average is based on quotes from John Hancock Insurance, MetLife, New York Life, Nationwide, and Pacific Life Insurance Company.

Table 1 works as follows: If, for example, you are a 65-year-old male and want to guarantee that income payments will continue for at least 10 years—even if you are not around to collect them—Table 1 shows that the (average) payout you can obtain is $519 per month, which is $6,228 per year, or 6.23% of a $100,000 premium. If you decide to buy (only) $75,000 worth of lifetime annuities, your income will be the same 6.23% of $75,000, which is $4,672 per year, or $389 per month. Similarly, if you want $1,000 of monthly income, you need to pay $192,616 ($12,000/0.0623) in premium. The ratio is maintained.

Now, if you want to squeeze a bit more yield, or income, from your $100,000 life annuity premium, you can dispense with the 10-year PC and select the 0-year PC. This choice is slightly riskier because if you die within 10 years (i.e., before the age of 75), the insurance company will not have to continue making any payment to you (obviously) or to your beneficiaries. In exchange for that risk, the company (or the average company) will be willing to pay $532 as opposed to $519 per month. The amount is an extra $156 per year as compensation for the extra risk. Now, whether that amount is worth it for you personally depends on your own circumstances and confidence in your health. But you

     ©2013 The Research Foundation of CFA Institute

probably would not be surprised to learn that most 65-year-olds who purchase a life annuity forfeit the extra $13 per month and select the 10-year PC. In fact, the research suggests that annuitants are selecting longer guarantee periods and other bells and whistles in exchange for reduced payment. Classical economists do not quite understand why people do this because they are thereby giving up the longevity pooling—which was the main point of buying the annuity. I will provide more discussion of this issue in the literature review in Chapter 3.

All of these numbers might seem overwhelming at first, but there are a number of important patterns in them you should note and understand. First, females consistently get less income than males do. For example, at age 65 (with a 10-year PC), a female gets only $497 compared with $519 for a male. The almost 5% difference is because females are expected to live longer than males. In this case, you can see mortality risk at work. Males assume more risk than females by purchasing a life annuity at age 65, and they get compensated for this risk. Note also that the older you are when you spend $100,000 on a life annuity, the more income you will receive. Again, the cause is mortality risk. In fact, the one overwhelming takeaway from the matrix in Table 1 is the way that mortality risk drives annuity quotes.

You might wonder how exactly an insurance company determines the appropriate payout rate to apply at different ages and genders, and that will be addressed in Chapter 2.

In conclusion, I remind the reader that the numbers in Table 1 are averages across a variety of insurance companies in late August 2012. Despite being a competitive market, some companies quoted higher rates and some quoted lower. The gap between companies can reach as high as 10% on any given day, which reflects various companies' appetite for the business. I will delve more into this issue when I discuss credit risk.

In the next section, I will establish why and how these rates have changed over time. Slightly more than a decade ago, all of the numbers in Table 1 were 50–75% higher, much to the chagrin of all retirees who are in the market to buy life annuities these days.

Q5. Historical Data: How Have Life Annuity Yields Changed over Time?

Sadly—at least for anyone in the market to buy—the payouts from life annuities were at a historical low as of August 2012. In fact, payouts have been in a long-term downtrend for decades, ever since interest rates peaked in 1981. Here is a case in point. In late August 2012, a 65-year-old female could receive $500 in monthly income from a 10-year PC life annuity in exchange for a $100,000 premium. (Remember that the $500 number—like most payouts I quote—is the average of the top five, or best, companies at the time.) Yet, a mere six years earlier, in August 2006, a 65-year-old female could have obtained $630 in monthly income for the exact same life annuity and premium. The difference is $130 per month and $1,560 per year. So, today's retiree, if he or she chooses to buy a life annuity, enjoys 20% less income than was available 6 years earlier and almost 50% less income than 15 years ago.[7] One can only sympathize with those who are annuitizing today versus a few years ago. Timing is everything.

I repeat just to be clear: For those who already purchased their annuities—5, 10, or 15 years ago—absolutely no change or reduction in their monthly income has occurred. They are entitled to whatever was promised to them at the time of purchase. It was guaranteed for life. The individual who purchases his or her annuity today is the one stuck with less income compared with a few years ago.

This decline or reduction in payouts has two causes. One is obvious, and the other is subtle. First and foremost, the downtrend is part of the story of low interest rates in a struggling global economy. Life annuities are similar to fixed-income coupon bonds, and just as the declining level of interest rates has increased bond prices over the last few years, so too have they *increased* the cost of life annuities. Remember, increasing the cost of a life annuity means that it costs more to generate the same income; that is, the annuitant receives less income for the same $100,000 premium. Ergo, payouts have dropped.

Note that back in the summer of 2006, well before the financial crises erupted in 2007 and 2008, the yield on a 10-year U.S. government bond was hovering around 5.20%. Thus, a $100,000 investment in this sort of bond would have generated coupons of $5,200 per year. But in late August 2012, the same risk-free government bond yield was closer to 1.5% and a $100,000 investment in the bond would yield only $1,500 per year in coupon income. The drop of almost 4 percentage points in bond yields is eventually transmitted to annuity prices. (I discuss the pricing of life annuities and the role of interest rates in much more detail in Chapter 2.) It is the big culprit, if you will, in the drop in income from life annuities. And although life annuity payouts are driven by many interest rates other than those on pure government bonds—for example, a mixture of mortgage rates and corporate bond rates—all of these rates are much lower than they were in 2006. Lower rates translate to lower payouts.

A more subtle reason for the decline in payouts over time has to do with longevity risk and population aging. One of the factors that determines how much an insurance company pays out on life annuities is its estimate or projection of how long annuitants might live. The longer it expects a cohort of 65-year-olds to live—that is, the longer it must continue making payments—the less it can afford to pay in exchange for the same $100,000 premium. Although detecting

---

[7]High yields have not been restricted to the late 1970s and early 1980s, when government bond interest rates were in double digits; in fact, in 1693, when the British government issued one of the first annuities to the public, the government offered 14% payouts.

or measuring population aging year over year is difficult, increases in life expectancy do have an impact over time. People are living longer, and payouts will be made for longer. In 2000, the typical 65-year-old would have been expected to live for 20 years; in 2010, perhaps 21 years. Insurance companies have been responding to this demographic change by (slowly) reducing the income they are willing to pay. Thus, even if interest rates had remained relatively constant for the last few years, the actual payouts on life annuities would have declined, although by a much smaller but hard-to-define amount.

Figure 1 displays historical payouts, expressed as an annualized percentage of the premium paid for males and females, for the eight years of 2004–2012. The figure also displays the yield on a risk-free 10-year U.S. government bond on the same dates. I selected the 10-year U.S. government bond rate as a proxy for general interest rates, but I am not suggesting that it is *the* rate that determines how insurance companies price annuities.

Figure 1. Life Annuity Payout Rate: Males vs. Females vs. 10-Year Treasury Rate, 2004–2012

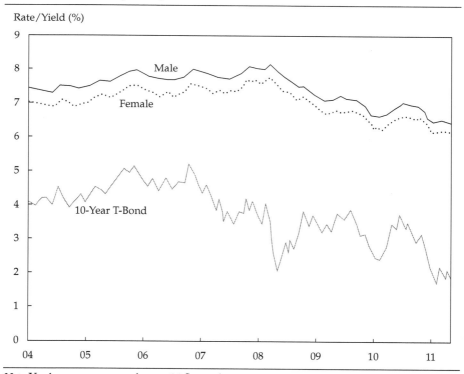

Note: Yearly measurements taken on 14 September.
Source: Data collected on a weekly basis from a variety of vendors and processed with the help of Cannex Financial Exchanges and the QWeMA Group.

A few things are worth noting in Figure 1, in addition to the obvious fact that males receive a higher yield than females because of their shorter longevity. First, as I mentioned earlier, the trend is noticeably downward over this period.

Second, life annuity payout rates are an average of 3.5 percentage points more than 10-year U.S. T-bonds, although this difference tends to be variable over time, especially during times of financial stress. So, the extra 3.5% is not a bad rule of thumb.

Third, and as important as the other two points, interest rates tend to be more volatile than life annuity payout rates. So, although the annuity rates do change regularly, they do not "bounce around" as much as market interest rates. Insurance companies are (probably) smoothing the ups and downs of market interest rates and taking their time in adjusting payouts in response. The exact mechanism by which this happens—and how exactly interest rates and longevity expectations are merged to create annuity payouts—is discussed in a number of papers mentioned in Chapter 2 and in the literature review of Chapter 3.

In summary, life annuity payouts change from week to week and often from day to day. Some companies offer better prices than others at different points in time or to retirees at different ages. The trend, however, is clear. Payouts today are much lower than they have been in the past, and unless interest rates move back to higher levels, payouts will continue to be depressed relative to historical averages.

Q6. How Is Life Annuity Income Taxed, and Is It Economically Neutral?

Benjamin Franklin is quoted as having said that nothing in life is certain other than death and taxes. Life annuities are a great example of both certainties. The income will eventually end upon the *death* of the annuitant, and the same income will indeed be *taxed*. Fortunately, however, not all of the income is fully taxable because some of the money you are receiving was yours already. In other words, some of the income will be excluded from taxes if you paid tax on the money previously and the income is fully yours. I will explain more about what this means in a moment, but first let me give a brief overview of retirement and income taxes.

When you buy a life annuity to generate income in retirement, the source of the funds—the origin of the $100,000 premium, for example—will affect the tax treatment of the income. There are really only two possible sources. First, the $100,000 you are using might come from a tax shelter, such as a 401(k), IRA, or other such account (in Canada, an RRSP or MP plan). When you use these funds to buy the annuity, you have carried out a *qualified* life annuity transaction. (In Canada, it would be called a "*registered* life annuity.")

Remember that the defining characteristic here is that you have never really paid any income tax on this qualified (registered) money yet. The money you contributed to the account was deducted from your taxable income—perhaps a long time ago—and you also never paid any income taxes on the gains as this money grew over time. For this reason, when you reach retirement around the age of 70 or so, you are required to start withdrawing money from these accounts and paying the income taxes you never paid when you were working and contributing.

Here is the bottom line: If you use that tax-sheltered money to purchase the life annuity, then all of the income from the annuity is taxable. Technically, you add this life annuity income to your other taxable income—such as pension income, employment income, or interest income—and pay whatever tax is due on the total amount every year.[8] Now, if you have little other income, or if you have large tax credits and/or deductions that you can take advantage of, you may end up paying very little tax. But 100% of the income is taxable. No exclusions or exemptions.

Alternatively, you can use a different pot of money to purchase a life annuity. The $100,000 premium might come from "regular" funds that are not part of a dedicated retirement tax shelter. This source buys you a *nonqualified* (*nonregistered* in Canada) annuity, and in this case, only a portion of the lifetime annuity income is taxable. After all, most of the money you are getting back was yours already and you have already paid tax on it. The actual amount that is taxable versus the nontaxable amount is determined by the insurance company that sells you the annuity on the basis of tax rules set forth by the U.S. Internal Revenue Service (IRS) or, in Canada, the Canada Revenue Agency (CRA).

Here is an example to help you understand the so-called *exclusion ratio* so that you can determine how much of the income will actually be taxable. The basic economic principle at work is a comparison of how much you invested in the life annuity (the $100,000 premium, for example) with how much you expect to receive from the life annuity. In other words, the tax rules depend on your life expectancy at the time of purchase and the number of payments you anticipate receiving. Note that the emphasis is on what you *expect* to happen, not what actually happens. The tax authorities wanted to keep things simple in this case and fix the amount that is taxable as opposed to varying it from year to year.

Say that, at the age of 65, you invested $100,000 in a life annuity that promises $550 per month, which is $6,600 per year, or a payout rate of 6.6%. According to the relevant IRS actuarial mortality table—which is a topic for another section—you can expect to live approximately 20 years from the age of 65. If you make it to 85 (and no more), you will receive $132,000 in total payments. Expectation is the key concept here. You are expecting $32,000 more than you paid. So, that is the amount of gain that is expected to be

---

[8]Some special age-based tax credits or deductions might be available on pension income, but they would be minor.

taxed. Of course, the IRS will not tax you on the $32,000 all at once, and it cannot wait until you die (at age 85) to get the tax on the $32,000, so it amortizes the amount over the remainder of your (expected) life. Each payment you receive is partially taxed in proportion to the ratio of 32 to 100. A portion of total income, however, is not taxable; that is, it is "excluded" from taxable income. For clarity, **Exhibit 4** provides an example of how the exclusion ratio is computed.

Exhibit 4.	How Much of Nonqualified Annuity Income Is Taxable?
Life annuity premium (investment)	$100,000
Age at time of purchase	65
Guaranteed monthly income for life	$550
Life expectancy in months (IRS tables)	240
Total amount of payments expected	240 × $550 = $132,000
Exclusion ratio	$100,000/$132,000 = 75.8%
Monthly income that is taxable[a]	(100% − 75.8%) × $550 = $133.33

[a]The entire $550 is taxable after you reach life expectancy, age 85.

One final wrinkle can make things a bit tricky in the United States with the exclusion ratio. Although the majority of the income you receive will not be taxable, this favorable treatment comes to an end once you reach your life expectancy and have received $132,000 in total payments. From that point onward, the entire income (which was $550 in the earlier example) is fully taxable. The exclusion ratio goes to zero, so to speak. The reason, or justification, is that every dollar you are now getting—after you reach age 85—is definitely more than you put in, so 100% of it is taxed. Your beneficiary can claim a tax credit, however, on your final (i.e., year of death) tax return if you did not recover your entire premium while still alive.

All these rules are a rather disconcerting and complicated way to tax income, and a number of economists—including, for example, Brown, Mitchell, Poterba, and Warshawsky (1999)—suggest some more-efficient alternatives. A few states in the United States also impose a small (0.5–3.0%) upfront premium tax when annuities are purchased with nonqualified funds, a fact that is also worth noting in the discussion of taxes.

Surprisingly, however, and in contrast to the United States, Canada's tax authorities allow you to continue to exclude the same portion of the life annuity income for as long as you live, even though you have received much more than your original premium back in payments. This treatment provides a generous tax break because the CRA uses outdated mortality tables that assume a lower life expectancy—especially when compared with the U.S. treatment, in which 100% of income becomes taxable at some point.[9]

Regardless of whether you use qualified or nonqualified funds and whether you have lived long beyond your life expectancy, part of your life annuity income will be considered taxable—regardless of where you live or the jurisdiction in which you reside. So, you must consider your tax situation in general and other taxable income in particular before choosing a life annuity for a retirement portfolio. And—all else being equal, if you have a choice—get your (taxable) life annuity in Canada if you do not mind receiving your income in Loonies.[10]

Q7. Who Sells Life Annuities (in North America), and How Are They Regulated?

Unlike opening a bank account, buying bonds from the U.S. Treasury, or participating in a dividend reinvestment plan (wherein you buy stock directly from a company), a life annuity is not bought directly from the product manufacturer. You cannot contact an insurance company via its toll-free number or on its website and then buy a life annuity from the company as you would a book, a pair of shoes, or an airline ticket. You must conduct the transaction through a licensed insurance agent. The agent is your financial intermediary for transacting with the insurance company. You give the agent your premium or investment, which the agent then gives to the insurance company, which then issues you the life annuity certificate or policy. In fact, buying a life annuity is similar to buying life insurance, which also must be done through a licensed agent. (There are exceptions to this rule; so-called term life insurance can be purchased from companies directly.)

Becoming a licensed insurance agent is not a complicated process. It usually involves a few months of study, an exam, and over time, some continuing education credits to retain the license. In the United States, the individual states administer and manage the process, and the end result is a Life and Health Insurance License. In Canada, agents must go through the Life License Qualification Program, which is a course of study, and then take an exam similar in scope and intent to the exam in the United States.

Note that a license to sell a life annuity (or any insurance for that matter) is quite different from an educational designation or qualification, such as a bachelor's degree, CFA or CFP (Certified Financial Planner) designation,

---

[9]At this point, I would like to offer a further disclaimer and suggest that you contact a tax specialist before making any irreversible decisions that might affect your taxes. The discussion in the text here is intended as a first view.

[10]"Loonie" is the nickname of the Canadian one-dollar coin.

or master's degree. Yes, a person might have learned a bit of finance, insurance, and economics in those programs, but to be able to actually sell a life annuity and to receive a commission on that sale, the agent needs the insurance license.

Just to be clear here, even if you call up a big life annuity company in the United States directly—such as New York Life or MetLife (or even an investment firm, such as Vanguard or Fidelity, for that matter)—and ask to buy a life annuity, it will refer you to an agent, possibly one of its own. You may seem to be bypassing the agent, but in fact, one is always in the background. Similarly, your financial adviser, broker, or wealth manager might be able to get you a life annuity but only if that person has an insurance license in addition to a securities (investment) license.

All of this information is more than just an institutional technicality. These licensing requirements have two implications in practice. The first is that someone locally (in the state or province itself) is regulating or overseeing sales practices. In fact, state insurance regulators review and approve the actual prices at which life annuities are sold. This effort should provide a measure of comfort in the purchase process. Among other requirements, agents must ensure that the life annuity is suitable or appropriate for the client before they recommend it.

Second, the existence of the insurance agent as an intermediary implies that this person will be compensated—probably via commission—for selling the life annuity. This commission can be anywhere from 0.5% to as much as 5% of the premium investment, depending on the company and product. Rest assured that this fee will be embedded in the quoted payout and paid by the insurance company to the insurance agent directly. So, you will not have to pay it separately or to the agent, but it will not be revealed to you either. One could argue that it should be disclosed and made transparent to the buyer, but that debate is for another book and time.

Moving on to the insurance companies themselves (the ones who manufacture, manage, and guarantee the annuity payments): They are also regulated by the insurance commissions. Every policy they issue, price they charge, or innovation they ponder must be approved by the commission. The justification for all of this red tape is that it provides a layer of scrutiny for the sole benefit of the consumer. No surprise, then, that the insurance industry is viewed as one of the most highly regulated businesses.

In return, during the financial crises of 2007–2008, state insurance regulators—especially the commissioner of insurance in New York—were extremely active in ensuring that policyholders were insulated and protected from emerging problems. In one case, a well-known national insurance company was attempting certain financial actions that could have benefited the owners and shareholders of the company but might have harmed the policy-holders themselves. In this high-profile case, the commissioner rode to the rescue and ensured that the widows and orphans and, for that matter, ordinary retirees would continue receiving their annuities. So, this regulation and oversight does occasionally have its upside.

Exhibit 5 lists the 12 largest insurance companies (according to their annuity reserves) in the United States that actively sell annuities—and not only life annuities. In addition to the various types of annuities they sell, each of these companies issues hundreds of millions of dollars of life insurance each year. Indeed, there are many types of annuities other than life annuities—which is discussed in another section—and the industry has come a long way from the old days of churches and parishes paying pensions. At the top of the list, MetLife is holding more than $278 billion worth of funds (known as reserves) that will eventually be used to pay annuities. The second-largest company in terms of annuity reserves is holding more than $179 billion in funds to pay these annuities.

Exhibit 5. Largest Life Insurers in the United States Ranked by Total Annuity Reserves Held as of 2010

Rank	Name	Total Annuity Reserves (millions)
1	MetLife	$278,089
2	TIAA-CREF	179,219
3	Prudential Financial	164,136
4	American International Group	157,048
5	Manulife Financial	146,525
6	ING North America	137,757
7	Hartford Life	129,629
8	Lincoln Financial	111,089
9	AXA Financial	99,725
10	AEGON SA	95,989
11	New York Life	81,721
12	Jackson National Life	79,172

Source: Based on ACLI tabulations of National Association of Insurance Commissioners data.

In summary, buying a life annuity is somewhat more complicated—and perhaps even more expensive—than going online and directly buying a bond ETF or term deposit. In the next section, I will explore what exactly the insurance company does with all the money it collects from annuitants, and the reserves it holds, while the retirees and annuitants wait to receive their monthly checks.

Q8. What Does the Insurance Company Do with the Premiums?

Insurance companies collect life annuity premiums from annuitants and must then invest the funds for many years, possibly decades, as they slowly pay out the lifetime income. As noted previously, the annuity reserves that insurance companies hold can amount to billions of dollars. It is natural to ask, therefore, what exactly they do with all this money. The issue is not simply a matter of curiosity; it concerns company solvency and regulation. After all, if the companies lose the money, not only is the annuitant affected but, given that those who are affected tend to be older and retired, so also is the public at large.

Rest assured that insurance regulators monitor and ensure that the funds are safely invested for the benefit of the annuitants, and the investments themselves are (also rather boring and) transparent. **Table 2** provides a snapshot of a typical insurance company investment (asset) portfolio. The data are from the NAIC, which is an umbrella organization and advocacy group consisting of all the various state insurance regulators in the United States.

Table 2. Percentage of Invested Assets by Size of Insurance Company Investment Assets

Asset Type	Big Companies (>$10 billion)	Small Companies (<$0.25 billion)
Corporate bonds	43.1%	36.1%
Structured securities	18.7	17.0
U.S. government bonds	18.2	35.1
Commercial mortgages	9.2	2.2
Corporate stocks	1.7	2.9
Other assets	9.1	6.7
Total	100.0%	100.0%

Source: Based on data from NAIC and Center for Insurance Policy and Research, "Capital Markets Special Report" (July 2011).

Table 2 reveals that most insurance company (admitted) assets are invested in bonds. A small fraction of assets—overall, less than 3% of the investment portfolio—is in common and preferred stocks. This tiny allocation to stocks—compared with what you or I might hold—is not by choice. Indeed, the companies are forced by regulators and by common economic sense to hold a conservative, safe portfolio.

Nevertheless, their investment portfolios are not, of course, immune from problems. After all, corporate bonds, mortgage bonds, and even government bonds do fluctuate in value, can default, and do have some economic risk associated with them. But the key is that these investment portfolios have low (stock market) betas. That is, the funds are not exposed to the vagaries of the stock market and protect current and future policyholders.

Another interesting insight from Table 2 is the difference between the holdings of large life insurance companies (those with investment assets greater than $10 billion) and the holdings of small insurance companies. Although some readers might expect small companies to have relatively riskier investment holdings, the opposite seems to be true. They actually hold more bonds, in general, and more U.S. government bonds, in particular. The implication is that smaller companies are probably earning less on their investment assets than the larger insurance companies. Are the bigger players in the industry perhaps "reaching for yield" by investing in riskier corporate and mortgage bonds with higher interest and coupon payments?

Needless to say, risk and reward are linked. Given their investment portfolios, the smaller insurance companies probably cannot offer as high a payout on life annuities because of their lower-yielding portfolios. Add this to the fact that consumers are less likely to trust a smaller insurance company to fulfill an income promise that might last decades, and it is not surprising that the life annuity business is dominated by large companies. (After all, it is not a year-by-year car insurance policy we are talking about; it is the retiree's livelihood.)

Note, however, that the numbers in Table 2 refer only to the insurance companies' own invested assets, also known as *general account* assets. The general account is where they deposit and comingle all of the annuity (and insurance) premiums they receive. The rates they offer on life (and other) annuities will partially depend on the current yield of these general account investments. If current bond yields are low, the companies clearly cannot afford to pay as much on new premium deposits. But an insurance company holds another type of account, the *separate account*, and in that account, anything goes.

In fact, insurance companies may be holding hundreds of billions of dollars in riskier assets, including domestic and international stocks, gold, commodities, real estate, and assorted mutual funds. But they are holding those assets as a custodian, guardian, or trustee and in the name of individual clients. They hold and manage them rather than own them, which is a subtle but big difference. These assets are not included in Table 2. They are quite separate.

To understand the separate account versus the general account, imagine having a bond certificate in your personal safety deposit box that is outright owned by you and, at the same time, a bond, a stock, or even a collection of gold coins that you are holding for a friend—but charging them a fee for this service, one that is perhaps even based on the value of the investments you are holding in trust. In both cases, the various investments are sitting in your safety deposit box, but the asset owned directly by you is analogous to an insurance company's general account assets; the assets that you are simply a guardian or trustee of would be separate account assets. Companies and their regulators must ensure that both accounts are kept safe and secure, but more is at stake in the general account.

In short, the investments an insurance company owns outright are conservative and tightly regulated. They cannot—and would not—take any chances investing the funds in risky or dubious assets. In fact, what they try to do is locate investments, such as bonds, that produce cash flows or coupons that match the payouts they are obligated to make. This mission is known as asset/liability matching and will be discussed more carefully in a later chapter.

At a simplistic level, an insurance company uses the life annuity premiums it receives from all the annuitants to purchase bonds. These bonds produce coupon income, which the insurance company then uses to pay the annuitants. Naturally, if you are not alive to get those annuity payments, the companies give them to the survivors. The key is for the insurance company's actuaries to figure out how long it will be paying the annuitants, in aggregate, so it can purchase bonds with the right maturities and durations.

First, however, consider what happens when insurance companies—and the investments they hold—run into financial difficulties.

Q9. Credit Risk: What Happens If the Company Goes Bankrupt?

Although insurance companies invest the premiums they receive conservatively, they do occasionally run into financial difficulties and sometimes a company goes bankrupt, is placed in receivership, or becomes insolvent. Most often, insurance regulators intervene before things get too bad and assist in transferring the policyholders' assets to a healthy insurance company that takes over the responsibilities. (I will explore this aspect in a moment.) If the intervention is carried out early enough, all can turn out well.

Yet, some spectacular insurance company blowups have occurred in the past few decades. For example, in August 1994, the fourth-largest insurance company in Canada (and one of the top 30 in North America) was taken over by regulators as it teetered on the edge of insolvency. The company was called Confederation Life, and its name lives on in infamy for anyone in the Canadian financial services industry. At the time, it had more than C$20 billion in assets, almost 5,000 employees (who lost their jobs), and more than 750,000 policyholders around the world. The main culprits in Confederation Life's failure were bad real estate investments and mortgage loans. Many commentators have blamed incompetent insurance company executives and regulators. McQueen (1997) provides an accessible and entertaining story of the demise of Confederation Life.

In another notable and publicized failure, which took place in September 1983, an insurance holding company by the name of Baldwin-United filed for Chapter 11 bankruptcy protection in the United States after insurance commissioners in Arkansas and Indiana took over management of its insurance subsidiaries. More than 165,000 policyholders had purchased high-yield annuities from Baldwin-United, and the money was frozen for more than three years while regulators and the courts picked up the pieces. The remaining assets were transferred to another insurance company.

What happened to Baldwin-United—originally, a maker of pianos—was that it extended itself far beyond its core competency (making pianos) by selling annuities and it promised yields that far exceeded what it was earning on the assets in its general account. This particular saga took years to resolve.

Another saga that has been ongoing for 20 years (yes, two decades) is Executive Life Insurance Company of New York. This New York City–based life insurer was placed in rehabilitation in April 1991 by the New York Superintendent of Insurance, who filed a petition for the liquidation of the company on 1 September 2011. The company's problem? A book of life annuities it took over from a DB pension plan.

Insurance company meltdowns are not limited to Canada or the United States either. In fact, one of the oldest insurance companies in the world, the Equitable Life Assurance Society, which was based in the United Kingdom and founded in the 18th century, had a large business selling investment plans with guaranteed annuity rates (GARs) attached. The GAR enabled savers to convert their accumulated money into a life annuity at a rate that was guaranteed in advance. So, for example, savers were guaranteed the ability to get 11% yields on their annuities regardless of actual interest rates and mortality rates (the ratio of deaths within a subgroup of the population expressed per 1,000 per year) at the time of annuitization. Because life annuity rates plummeted in the late 1990s, Equitable Life faced serious financial difficulties and then tried to renege on the GAR promises. The result was that, in 2000, it had to (effectively) close down for business. To those familiar with the lingo, the company had sold "naked put options" but had never bothered to hedge or reinsure them.

The insurance industry has (hopefully) learned from these disasters.

Moreover, although these disasters were reported extensively in the media at the time, I would like to point out that the situation in general is not as bad or scary as it sounds from such headlines. Nowadays, annuitants and policyholders are protected by guarantee funds. Even if your insurance company goes bankrupt and general creditors (unsecured bondholders) lose their money, the chance is good that you and the other annuitants will get most of your promised income from other insurance companies.

State Guarantee Associations. The National Organization of Life and Health Insurance Guaranty Associations (NOLHGA) is a voluntary association made up of the life and health insurance guaranty associations of all 50 states, the District of Columbia, and Puerto Rico. The organization was founded in 1983, when the state guaranty associations determined that a need existed for a mechanism to help coordinate their efforts to protect policyholders when a life or health insurance company insolvency affected people in many states. Basically, the mechanism is that when something goes wrong, the stronger insurance companies in the industry pool their resources and rescue the weaker company. It is similar to Federal Deposit Insurance Corporation (FDIC) or Canada Deposit Insurance Corporation insurance that protects bank depositors. Although there are some important differences between "state guarantee funds" and the banking industry's version, they perform the same function.

The individual state guarantee funds in the United States have a parallel organization in Canada called "Assuris." **Exhibit 6** provides a brief overview of what is covered and how to obtain more information about the limits.

Exhibit 6. Guarantees and Protections Available to Life Annuitants

United States: State Guarantee Funds	Canada: Assuris
Between $80,000 and $500,000 premium coverage, depending on the state in which the annuitant lives and the insurance company is domiciled.	Policy to be transferred to a solvent company with the guarantee that annuitant will retain greater of $2,000 per month or 85% of the promised monthly income benefit.

Notes: These entities are funded by insurance companies collectively, not governments. More information can be found at www.nolhga.com and www.assuris.ca.

NOLHGA has been active recently in the following instances: when Golden State Mutual Life Insurance was shut down by regulators in California in September 2009; when Shenandoah Life entered receivership in Virginia in February 2009; when Standard Life Insurance Company of Indiana was taken over by Indiana regulators in December 2008; and when London Pacific Life & Annuity Company was liquidated in July 2004. None of these events, managed and coordinated with the help of NOLHGA, were pleasant for policyholders, but policyholders were eventually compensated for some of their losses.

©2013 The Research Foundation of CFA Institute

As far as the frequency of financial disasters is concerned, although hundreds, if not thousands, of banks have failed (in the United States) over the last decade, fewer than 10 annuity carriers have been taken over by the state insurance regulators, and they have been small ones. So, the risk is certainly present, but it is not as severe as in the banking industry.

In summary, insurance companies can run into financial distress, and despite the fact that regulators and guarantee funds are available to smooth things out in times of distress, the reluctance of (potential) policyholders to invest or deposit more than the protected limits in any one company's policy is understandable. Indeed, the concept of diversification applies not only to stocks and bonds but also to insurance policies, including life annuities. The next section describes how default risk and the credit rating of an insurance company can affect how much life annuities pay out.

Q10. Do the Credit Ratings of the Insurance Company Affect Payouts?

Although policyholders are protected by the state-mandated guarantee funds in the United States (Assuris in Canada), there is a strict limit on how much is actually covered. So, if your life annuity premium is above the limit, you are "at risk" if the company runs into financial distress. Moreover, even if your premium is under the limit—which means you are 100% covered, in principle—the possibility always exists of delays in regulatory resolution or unwanted personal stress from the corporate distress. Therefore, as you might expect in a well-functioning capital market, riskier companies—in terms of their overall credit ratings—do actually pay out more on life annuities. The effect is akin to corporate bonds paying higher yields than government bonds or banks of different risks paying different rates on savings accounts, even though they are all covered by the FDIC. Default risk (and stress) matters.

Here is an example. On 20 September 2012, a 65-year-old male was quoted a life annuity of $527 per month (on a $100,000 premium with a 10-year PC) from the insurance company Genworth Life. The same individual was only offered $507 per month, however, from New York Life. In other words, Genworth was offering an extra $20 per month for the same $100,000 premium, which is $240 per year, or 4% more income, than New York Life. This difference is not trivial. So, why was one company paying more than the other? Are not these life annuity payouts a commodity? Given how easy it is to search for prices online, would not everyone go to Genworth for the extra $240 per year? Part of the answer, as demonstrated in **Exhibit 7**, is credit risk.[11] Genworth is, in actuality or is at least perceived to be, a riskier company—especially compared with New York Life—and, therefore, must compensate the buyer with a better payout.

By riskiness, I do not mean volatility of the company's stock price (in the sense of, for example, having a higher beta); indeed, New York Life stock is not publicly traded. I am referring to the overall creditworthiness of the company as evaluated by independent credit rating agencies. These agencies focus on such issues as the following: Will the company be able to pay its debts on time? Does it have riskier investments backing its liabilities? The bottom line is that New York Life is a safer company than Genworth. So, it does not have to pay out as much.

Exhibit 7.   Monthly Income vs. Credit Rating, 20 September 2012

Rank	Insurance Company	Income for Male at Age 75	A.M. Best Credit Rating
1	Genworth	$676.30	A
2	American National	670.37	A
3	MetLife	662.98	A+
4	Nationwide	660.89	A+
5	Lincoln Financial	658.85	A+
6	Guardian	658.65	A++
7	New York Life	658.50	A++
8	Integrity Life Insurance (W&S)	655.64	A+
9	Principal Financial Group	653.54	A+
10	John Hancock	645.90	A+
11	Minnesota Life	645.19	A+
12	Pacific Life	644.45	A+
13	Symetra Life Insurance	640.66	A
14	Hartford Life	631.95	A
15	Lincoln Benefit Life Insurance	631.25	A+
16	Jackson National Life	614.91	A+
17	Protective Life Insurance	613.04	A+
18	American General Life	610.97	A
	Average	$646.34	

Source: Based on data from Cannex Financial Exchange.

In the United States, there are three well-known credit rating agencies. They are Moody's Investors Service, Standard & Poor's (S&P), and A.M. Best. And although Moody's and S&P have higher visibility and greater

---

[11]Other reasons may be at work, of course, in the difference between what Genworth Life and New York Life are offering. Genworth Life may have lower operating expenses or may be more competitive; maybe it wants the business and is trying harder. But credit risk is probably the main factor.

name recognition, when it comes to insurance companies, A.M. Best is the more comprehensive and widely cited. As Exhibit 7 shows, the A.M. Best rating of Genworth is a single A whereas the rating for New York Life is A++, two notches better.

Note in Exhibit 7 that, in general, the A++ companies do not offer the best rates, although the risk-versus-payout relationship is not perfect: The highest payout for a 75-year-old man was from Genworth's and the lowest payout was from American General Life, although both companies—with a difference of more than $60 per month and $720 per year—had the same A.M. Best rating.

Nevertheless, the A++ company is highly unlikely to ever be paying the most, which is almost axiomatic if you think about it. In fact, in a formal statistical regression of the highest monthly life annuity payout (the dependent variable) on credit ratings (the independent variable), the relationship is statistically significant and the slope is negative (with a p-value of 7%). Higher-rated companies pay less. **Figure 2** displays this relationship in a graphical format.

Figure 2.   Relationship between Credit Rating and Annuity Payout

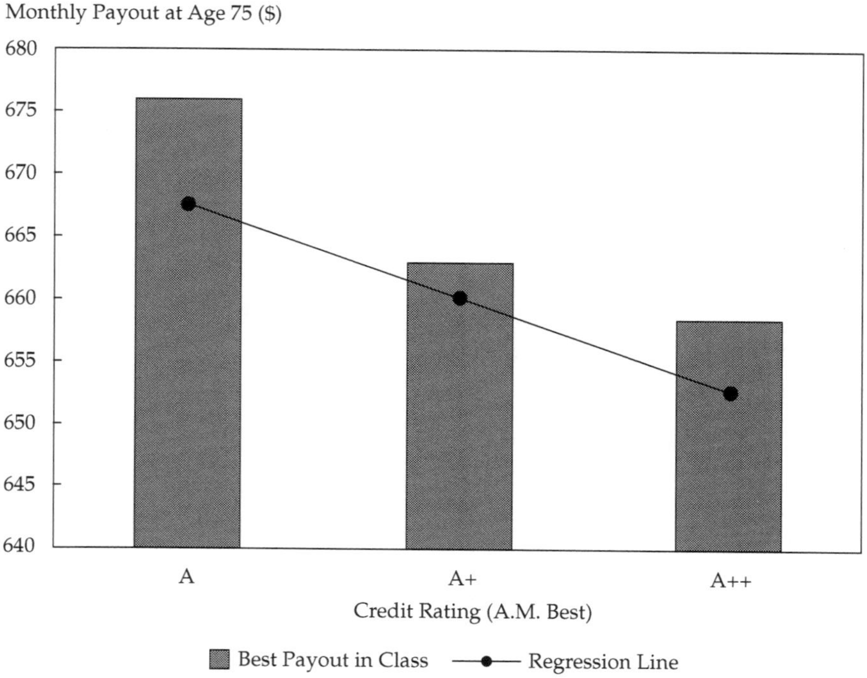

Monthly Payout at Age 75 ($)

Digging a bit deeper into the financial economics of the matter provides a good reason why higher-rated companies must pay out less on life annuities than lower-rated companies do. Consider why a rating agency would rate Genworth lower than New York Life. Recall that insurance companies back, or hedge, their life annuities (and life insurance) with similar investments in their general accounts. Some companies have general account investments that are safer than others—mortgages and corporate bonds—and that greater safety leads to a higher credit rating. Lower-risk bonds tend to offer lower yields. Therefore, the companies with higher credit ratings, and lower-yielding assets, cannot afford to pay as much on their life annuities.

In the spirit of chicken-and-egg theorizing of which came first, you can debate whether the higher-rated insurance companies decided to purchase the lower-yield assets or whether it was the other way around—they get a higher rating because of their lower-yielding (and safer) portfolios—but the end result is the same.

When you purchase a life annuity, you have a choice of more than 20 insurance companies offering what is essentially a commodity product. The only economic difference between a lifetime of cash from Company A and from Company B is their chances of experiencing financial difficulties during your life. This risk is reflected in the life annuity payout rate.

Remember, however, that if you keep your purchase under the state guarantee fund limits—$100,000 in most states—your income is protected even if the company defaults on its (other) obligations. So, in some sense, credit rating should not matter to you. You might as well go with the highest cash flow. Of course, those planning to annuitize larger sums than a guarantee fund limit might want to put the whole amount in the safer company to avoid the difficulty of managing a large number of vendors simply to keep individual purchases under the state limits.[12]

Q11. A First Look at Methuselah Risk: What If Annuitants Lived for 969 Years?

The Old Testament makes reference to Methuselah, the grandfather of Noah, who lived to the ripe old age of 969 years and was the oldest person mentioned in what is known as the Hebrew Bible. The modern-day recordholder for longevity as of September 2012 was Jeanne Louise Calment, who was born on 21

---

[12]I personally would probably forgo the extra $20 per month and stick to the A++ company with my nest egg. I would hate to see my annuity provider in the financial headlines for the wrong reasons, even if I am 100% covered. As any behavioral economist will remind you, peace of mind is hard to quantify.

February 1875 and died on 4 August 1997. She was French—which may or may not explain her extreme longevity—and lived a total of 122 years and 164 days. A far cry from 969, but impressive nevertheless.[13]

We do not know whether she ever purchased a life annuity from an insurance company—although she did benefit financially from her longevity—but the thought of having a Methuselah or even a Jeanne Calment among their annuitants has struck fear into the hearts of insurance company executives from time immemorial. What if people live longer than anticipated by the actuaries? What happens if scientists find a cure for cancer or diabetes? Would insurance companies be able to afford to pay annuitants for that much longer? Would it place the company at risk?[14]

Some research a few years ago conducted by insurance analysts at Moody's, in which I participated, sheds some light on the matter.[15] **Table 3** displays the main results from their analysis and report. It provides some indication of what might happen to company profitability (and credit risk) if certain diseases were cured, mortality were reduced, and annuitants lived longer than anticipated. Here is an example of how to interpret Table 3.

Table 3.   How Reductions in Mortality Affect Annuity Profitability

		Unisex 55		Unisex 62		Unisex 70	
Mortality	Reduction	Life Exp.[a]	Spread (bps)	Life Exp.[a]	Spread (bps)	Life Exp.[a]	Spread (bps)
Status quo	0%	82.9	+100	83.8	+100	85.6	+100
Stroke and pneumonia	−10	83.8	+85	84.7	+77	86.4	+60
Cancer and diabetes	−40	87.4	+39	88.1	+4	89.4	−67
Heart disease	−80	97.7	−36	97.9	−111	98.6	−257

[a]Expectancy.

Notes: The table displays the *ex post* spread calculated from a Moody's model that would be earned from an immediate annuity block of business assuming an *ex ante* desired spread of 100 bps.
Source: Based on data from Robinson and Fliegelman (2002).

---

[13]Jeanne Calment and longevity risk will be forever linked by the fact that she engaged in the peculiar French practice of selling her apartment with the proviso that the buyer could occupy it upon the seller's death. She sold it in 1965 at the age of 90 to a 47-year-old man who, despite living 30 more years, did not outlive her.
[14]Some insurance companies (such as TIAA-CREF in the United States) offer *participating annuities*, in which the company is entitled to reduce payment to all retirees in the event of a greater-than-expected increase in longevity. This tontine-like provision is rare; most companies are on the hook for the payments.
[15]Recall that Moody's is one of the main credit rating agencies in the United States, so naturally, this sort of question preoccupies them.

Consider an insurance company that sells a life annuity to a 55-year-old and prices the annuity so that it makes a profit or spread of 100 bps (i.e., 1%; a basis point is 0.01%). What this 100 bp spread means is that when the insurance company is pricing the annuity, if the assets in the general account earn 5%, for example, it expects to pay out 4% to the annuitant and keep the spread. Basically, they keep 1 percentage point of the investment return on assets as a profit margin.

Now, assume that scientists were able to completely eliminate all deaths from strokes and pneumonia, which, according to biostatisticians, would reduce mortality rates across the board by 10% at all ages. In this case, according to the analysts' model reported in Table 3, life expectancy at age 55 would increase by about 1 year, from 82.9 to 83.8. Obviously, the insurance company would end up paying more in aggregate to its annuitants, but the realized profit would be reduced only to 0.85%. In other words, the companies would still earn a profit but not as much as they had previously. In fact, continuing with the same logic, even if cancer and diabetes were completely eliminated, the realized spread would drop to 0.39% but still be positive. What this means is that, even if life expectancy at age 55 jumped from 82.9 to 87.4, the insurance company could still earn an *ex post* profit.

This sort of theoretical exercise rests on many assumptions that are too numerous to mention (I know because I helped create the model Moody's used), but there are some important takeaways from this simple thought experiment. First, notice the columns labeled "Unisex 55," "Unisex 62," and "Unisex 70" in Table 3. When the company sells a life annuity to a 55-year-old, it exposes itself to less risk than when it sells the annuity to a 62-year-old or 70-year-old. But if mortality is reduced suddenly and unexpectedly, this change will have a greater impact on companies with older annuitants. Consider: If the company was expecting to make payments for 20 years, on average, and it had to make them for 22 years, the relative increment of 10% is not great. But if the company was expecting to make payments for eight years, on average, that extra two years of longevity translates into 25% more payments. Remember also that the company is paying the 70-year-old much more relative to the 55-year-old, so this shock (extra years of payments) can definitely hurt profitability. The main result shown in Table 3, however, is that the impact of the changes would not be as dramatic as you might expect, at least for annuities sold to young individuals.

Another important point worth noting relates to the fact that life insurance and life annuities create opposing liabilities. When it comes to the risk of selling annuities to Mr. Methuselah, if you also sold him a sizable life insurance policy, your overall risk exposure would be neutralized. Yes, the company would have to make life annuity payments for 969 years, but then again, it would not have to pay out death benefits for 969 years. What the company lost on the life annuity side, it might gain on the life insurance side. Moreover, although the insurance company may not have sold life insurance and life annuities to the same Methuselah, as long as the shock to mortality affects an equal number of life insured and life annuitants, the effect would be the same: One change offsets the other. This effect assumes, of course, that the insurance company has an equal and equivalent dollar exposure to life insurance and life annuities across the same age groups, but the main idea holds true even if it does not. This effect, by the way, is called a "natural hedge" and effectively implies that Methuselah risk is not as scary as it sounds if the insurance company has a balanced portfolio of "long" and "short" longevity risks.

Q12. Are Life Annuities Popular, and What Is the Size of the U.S. Market?

Life annuities can be viewed as either extremely popular or highly unpopular depending on your perspective and definition of "annuity." For example, if you consider DB pensions—government pensions, social security programs, and the like—to be life annuities, then they are one of the most successful products (and programs) in financial history. According to the U.S. Social Security Administration, almost 39 million retired Americans and their dependents collected more than $45 billion dollars in benefits during one month (December 2011) alone. The $1,234 average monthly benefit received adds up to more than a *half a trillion* dollars in annual life annuity income.

The Canadian Pension Plan—which is equivalent to Social Security but much less generous than the American version—pays $28 billion annually to 5 million retired Canadians and their dependents, an average of $530 per month.

In any given year, thousands of retirees who are part of a corporate or public DB pension plan exit the labor force and actively select the annuity option instead of the lump sum. Indeed, you cannot get better examples of the masses enjoying their life annuities.

In contrast to the publicly mandated and employment pension programs, however, the voluntary life annuity market in North America is small. In fact, even in the universe of all annuities sold, life annuities are but a small fraction. **Table 4** provides an indication of the size of this market in relative and absolute terms. It displays the volume of sales (i.e., premiums contributed by individuals) during a 12-month period and breaks down the numbers across three broad annuity categories. The "fixed immediate annuities" category includes our coveted life annuities.

Table 4. Total Sales of U.S. Individual Annuities, Year Ending 30 June 2012

Product Type	Sales (billions)	Percent of Sales
Variable annuity	$150.7	68.2%
Fixed deferred annuity (including book, market, and indexed)	61.5	27.8
Fixed immediate annuity (including life annuities)	8.9	4.0
Total for 12 months	$221.1	100.0%

Source: Based on data from the Insured Retirement Institute (September 2012). Data are from 55 insurance companies reporting.

At this point, I do not want to get lost in the details of the other annuities listed in Table 4, which deserve their own sections; what follows is a brief description of the broad categories.

A *variable annuity* (VA), which is the largest category of annuity when ranked by sales in the United States, is essentially a mutual fund (or a collection of funds) with some added insurance and financial guarantees. Some industry participants will disagree with this simple description of a VA, but you will have to trust me here, especially if this is your introduction to these instruments. VAs are not really life annuities in any way that an insurance or financial economist would accept. And although the insurance industry's own regulators and lawyers might consider them annuities, they are best described as savings and accumulation products with, at most, an *option* to convert the product into an income stream eventually. So, if and when a VA is actually converted into income, it would be properly described as a life annuity. Until that time, it is a savings and accumulation vehicle. (I will discuss more about VAs later.)

Moreover, few VAs end up being converted (annuitized) into lifetime income streams. In most cases, they are cashed out, surrendered, or exchanged for other annuities. Statistics from LIMRA (2010) indicate that only 1–3% of variable annuities are ever annuitized.[16] So, they are called "annuities," but they are very different from the life annuity with a 2,500-year history. Do not confuse them.

As Table 4 shows, 68.2% of total "annuity" sales during the year were VAs. It is the largest segment of the annuity market (and perhaps deserving of its own book).

Fixed deferred annuities (FDAs) were 27.8% of sales. These products also are primarily savings instruments in which individuals deposit premiums and collect some form of interest gains, but unlike VAs, the funds in FDAs (1) are

---

[16]LIMRA is the Life Insurance Management Research Association (located in Windsor, Connecticut).

©2013 The Research Foundation of CFA Institute

placed in the insurance company's general account and (2) do not fluctuate on the basis of the stock market. Think of this category as the insurance company equivalent of a safe bank deposit but perhaps one in which the interest rate is slightly better than that offered by the bank. The FDA category also contains the *option* to convert into income. But as with the VA, few FDAs are annuitized, or converted into an income stream. They are purchased primarily as accumulation or savings vehicles and then usually cashed out in full. FDAs are often viewed as a type of tax-deferred certificate of deposit, which are sold by banks and credit unions.

Finally, the category that is most relevant to this book is the *fixed immediate annuity*. As its name suggests, it is an annuity guaranteeing, or promising, an actual income, usually starting immediately. During the 12-month period ending 30 June 2012, a total of only $8.9 billion of these fixed immediate annuities were sold in the United States. This is a mere 4% of the $221 billion total annuity sales and—at best—13% of fixed annuity (FDA plus fixed immediate annuity) sales.

Moreover, what fraction of the $8.8 billion flowed into (true) life annuities, in which payments are guaranteed for the remainder of an individual's or couple's life, is not easy to determine because the data are not available. Recall that some annuities are purchased for a term certain that is not necessarily a lifetime. Nevertheless, anecdotal evidence and discussions with industry experts indicate that at least three-quarters of these sales are true lifetime contracts, perhaps with PC or refunds attached. More granularity is difficult to obtain. (I hope that the industry—or at least some of the larger companies—will release a more refined breakdown of the broad category of fixed immediate annuities.)

In summary, annuities, broadly construed, are a multi-billion-dollar, perhaps trillion-dollar, business. Social Security and pension programs are essentially life annuities. The amount of money flowing into life annuities issued by insurance companies, however, is small. It is small relative to the size of Social Security and DB pensions, and it is small relative to the size of the overall insurance company annuity market. It is only 4% of insurance company annuity sales.

So, from a statistical point of view, if you happen upon someone who just purchased an "annuity policy" from an insurance company, there is a 96% chance it is not the type of annuity I have been discussing and advocating in this book.

Q13. Is a Variable Annuity with a Guaranteed Lifetime Withdrawal Benefit a Substitute for a Life Annuity?

As I mentioned in the previous section, tax-deferred VAs, which are the bulk of the annuity market in the United States, were initially promoted for the favorable tax treatment and death guarantees they enjoyed. As these products have moved to include guarantees of minimum income streams that investors could receive, however, those features have become critical selling points. In this section, I will address the most popular type of income guarantee—the guaranteed lifetime withdrawal benefit (GLWB). A VA product that contains this guarantee often competes with a life annuity.

A GLWB rider on a VA allows the investor to lock in a minimum income for life—similar to a life annuity or deferred income annuity—without surrendering the capital irreversibly. Thus, these riders provide some of the retirement longevity protection of a traditional annuity without surrendering upside potential or liquidity. The best way to think of them is as a relatively more expensive mutual fund with a complex path-dependent put option that allows for a minimal withdrawal level. The guaranteed withdrawal level is less than what a life annuity would offer, although the difference may not seem huge on first examination. A GLWB might permit withdrawals of 5% for life, whereas a life annuity issued to the same buyer at the same time might pay 7% or 8% for life. **Exhibit 8** provides an outline of the differences between a traditional life annuity and a VA with a GLWB.

Exhibit 8. Comparison of a Life Annuity with a VA + GLWB

Element	Traditional Life Annuity	VA + GLWB
Liquidity	Little liquidity, especially in the event of no PC guarantee.	Possible surrender charges, but the account can always be liquidated.
Payout rate	Function of age and interest rates.	Lower than a life annuity by 1.5–2.0 percentage points.
Costs and fees	Embedded commissions and fees are on the order of 1–2% of the premium.	Various layers of fees within the VA are difficult to disentangle, but generally 1–3% of assets annually.
Other	Primary focus of this research monograph.	A shrinking number of insurance companies are offering this product.

Here is a synopsis of the mechanics of the VA plus GLWB: The individual policyholder deposits, or rolls over from another VA, a sum of money into an investment portfolio that is then allocated into a number of subaccounts that contain stocks, bonds, and other generic investments. The portfolio then grows (or shrinks) over time, depending on the performance of the underlying investments. Any capital gains are tax deferred and eventually treated as ordinary income. (In Canada, there is no tax deferral of gains.) Up to this point, it might sound like a mutual fund.

©2013 The Research Foundation of CFA Institute

Then, at some future date—which is usually under the control of the policyholder—the annuitant can start taking guaranteed withdrawals from the account. Think of this income as a systematic withdrawal plan (SWiP) at a nominal (i.e., not inflation-adjusted), nondecreasing level.[17] The income is guaranteed to never decline for the remaining life of the annuitant and, in the case of a joint product, of the annuitant's (younger) spouse. Thus, in contrast to a SWiP, if the annuity's underlying investment portfolio (that is, the account value) ever reaches zero, the guaranteed income will continue so long as one member of the couple is still alive.

The guaranteed withdrawal rate is determined by the insurance company issuing the GLWB at the time of sale. The guarantee amount is the product of multiplying a guaranteed rate by the guaranteed base and is determined at the point of first withdrawal. Moreover, if the investment portfolio happens to grow even while undergoing these withdrawals, the guaranteed base might reset to a higher level and hence generate even greater withdrawals. As far as estate values are concerned, upon the second death, whatever is left over in the account goes to the heirs, with the requisite tax implications depending on the cost basis (and depending on whether the GLWB was inside a tax shelter).

GLWBs as thus described exist in a variety of alternative formats and are often bundled with an array of other guarantees, ratchets, or step-ups linked to death benefits and life insurance (all of which are beyond the scope of this book). Regardless of the specifics, however, the basic GLWB ensures that some withdrawals will continue for life regardless of whether the underlying account has the funds to support them. In other words, fees and periodic withdrawals are deducted from the VA account as long as there are funds available there. But if those periodic withdrawals ever fully deplete this account, the underwriter steps in and funds the remaining withdrawals for the lifetime of the investor.

The periodic withdrawals provide downside protection, but some upside potential remains for the underlying account to grow if markets perform well. The investor preserves liquidity, because the underlying account value

---

[17]A SWiP is a (dumb) mechanical liquidation rule that extracts a fixed amount of cash from a retirement portfolio by selling assets to create a desired level of income, regardless of the price level of markets. So, for example, if a retiree implements a SWiP for $50,000 per year and, in one particular year, the dividends and interest from the portfolio are (only) $20,000, then $30,000 worth of securities are sold to make up the income difference. Under a SWiP, the systematic sale of $30,000 worth of securities ignores fundamental valuation levels and any other market-timing rules. It is the mirror image of dollar-cost averaging, under which a fixed amount of money is invested in securities on a regular basis independent of valuation levels. Although many individuals view SWiPs as an alternative to life annuities, a SWiP can fully deplete the portfolio whereas a life annuity cannot. The GLWB offers a SWiP with some insurance protection—namely, that if the account value ever hits zero as a result of the depletions, the insurance company will continue paying the annuity.

may be withdrawn at any time (minus any surrender charges). Unlike a traditional life annuity, if the investor dies, his or her heirs inherit the remaining account value.

The insurance companies manufacturing the relatively new generation of VAs with a GLWB view the product as a private-sector replacement for DB pensions in an increasingly DC world. Whether the GLWB is better than the life annuity from the consumer's perspective depends on a complex relationship between the pricing of the guarantee, the retiree's optimal consumption strategy, and the existence of bequest motives.

In summary, although a smaller group of insurance companies are offering them, the latest generation of VA contracts has been financially engineered to provide an assortment of lifetime income guarantees that are meant to protect the policyholder against what the industry has termed "sequence of returns risk" and "longevity risk." These terms refer to the chance that a retirement portfolio from which cash is being withdrawn will suffer early losses and/or the retiree will live longer than average. The common denominator of all these insurance riders is that they contain an implicit put option on financial markets plus some form of longevity insurance, akin to a pure life annuity. Of course, using the concept of put–call parity, they can also be viewed as call options to annuitize at some variable strike price. The (anecdotal) "sales pitch" for these products revolves around the idea that the guarantees permit investors to take on more investment risk than they would without the guarantees.[18]

Here is the bottom line: To the naked eye, the VAs with GLWB might appear to have all the benefits of a life annuity—guaranteed income, risk pooling—but without the costs associated with illiquidity and irreversibility. However, although the GLWB product has merits, especially considering the research evidence that it was initially underpriced, it is not a substitute for pure life annuities because of its lower yields. For example, whereas a life annuity might pay 6% to a 65-year-old, the GLWB rate under the same market conditions would be in the vicinity of 4%.

---

[18]A paper by Milevsky and Kyrychenko (2008) seems to indicate that, indeed, investors do take on more risk when these riders are provided.

2. Ten Formulas to Know

In this chapter, I address the 10 main formulas that researchers use and that practitioners should know in the life annuity literature.

Q14. What Is a Biological Mortality Rate, and How Is It Measured?

When an insurance company issues or sells you a life annuity, the company must try to predict when you will die, and payments will cease, so that it can determine the appropriate monthly payments. Naturally, the longer an annuitant is forecast to live—and the lower the annuitant's *mortality rate*—the lower the payments must be. For example (with interest and the time value of money ignored), if the annuitant is forecast to die in exactly 10 years, then the $100,000 annuity premium must be returned to the annuitant in (only) 120 installments, which is $833 (100,000/120) per month (with interest ignored), but if the annuitant is forecast to die in exactly 15 years, then the monthly payment must be lower, $556 (100,000/180). So, pricing annuities is mostly about predicting how long annuitants will live and payments will be made.

How does the insurance company make these predictions? What happens if it gets it wrong and you do not die exactly when you were supposed to?

The answer to the first question is, of course, that because the insurance companies are selling many life annuities to many different people, they do not have to predict *exactly* how long you will live but, rather, how long an individual member of a group will live *on average*. And forecasting the life expectancy of a group is much easier than forecasting the exact length of life for any one individual.

For example, suppose Client 5 lives beyond the group's life expectancy, but Client 17 does not make it to the group's life expectancy. The more-than-average number of payments made to Client 5 will be offset by the fewer-than-average number of payments made to Client 17. (The client numbers are completely arbitrary, and perhaps two shorter-lived annuitants—Clients 17 and 8—will offset one very long-lived annuitant—Client 5—but the idea is the same.)

What makes this principle of offsetting risks work in an accurate manner is the so-called *law of large numbers*. If the insurance company pools a large enough number of annuitants with similar forecasted life expectancies, the risk-offsetting process can take place with much more accuracy than would be possible for a pool of just two or three people. Obviously, selling one annuity to each of two 65-year-olds in the hope that they will cancel each other is a silly gamble. But if the company sells thousands of life annuities to a group in their 60s, then the law of large numbers guarantees that, *on average*, even though not in any individual case (except by coincidence), they really will live to their life expectancy. So, all the insurance actuary has to worry about is the behavior of the average in the pool.[19] For this task, historical mortality patterns of similar groups are helpful.

In fact, to be even more precise, insurance actuaries do not necessarily focus on the life expectancy of the group but on year-by-year mortality rates. In this manner, they can mix and match people of different ages in their large annuity pool with the same risk-offsetting result applying on a year-by-year basis.

Equation 1 displays the definition of a one-year mortality rate:

$$q_x = \frac{\text{No. dying between age } x \text{ and age } (x+1)}{\text{No. alive at age } x}. \tag{1}$$

Now, my objective is not to convert the reader into an insurance actuary or to delve too deeply into the actuarial minutiae, but for clarity, **Table 5** displays historical mortality rates for a homogenous group of annuitants who purchased life annuities from insurance companies in the past few decades. Note that the table is based on a group's (past) realized experience, but the data are then used, with slight modifications, to forecast current experience.[20]

Table 5. Annuitant Mortality Table for Various Ages

Death between Ages	Female Rate (q_x)	Male Rate (q_x)
55 and 56	0.00246	0.00453
60 and 61	0.00386	0.00643
65 and 66	0.00625	0.00994
70 and 71	0.01003	0.01698
75 and 76	0.01756	0.02830
80 and 81	0.03193	0.04604
85 and 86	0.05791	0.07328
90 and 91	0.10176	0.11221

Source: Based on data from the Society of Actuaries, an organization in the United States that, among other responsibilities, tabulates and reports various types of mortality tables; "Annuity 2000 Mortality Table" (www.SoA.org).

---

[19]For a much more precise and proper mathematical definition of how the risk is reduced with a large number of annuitants, please see the actuarial references mentioned in Chapter 3.
[20]In simple terms, this table can be described as a *static* mortality table, one without any mortality improvement projections, as opposed to a *dynamic* mortality table, in which a particular cohort is modeled over time.

Here is how to interpret the numbers in Table 5. Based on historical patterns for a large group of individuals who purchased annuities, 1.003% of 70-year-old women died before reaching their 71st birthday. This fact can be used to forecast that the probability a 70-year-old female will die before her 71st birthday is 0.01003 or 1.003%.

Here is another way of viewing Table 5. Given a large group of 70-year-old females, the expectation is that 1% of them will die prior to their 71st birthday and that the other 99% will survive to their 71st birthday. So, if the insurance company has to pay each 71-year-old woman $1,000 at the end of the year, it needs to charge only $99,000 to a group of 100 70-year-old women. This $990 is charged to any individual member of the group at the beginning of the year (again, interest is ignored). The company does not know who the 1% will be, but it is irrelevant. All the company needs is the average, so it can figure out how much to charge the group as a whole.

If you look carefully at the mortality rates in Table 5, you will notice a steadily increasing pattern, at the rate of between 9% and 11% per year for both males and females. In other words, the mortality rate during age $(x + 1)$ is approximately 9–11% higher than the mortality rate during age x. Were it not for this "law" of mortality—and if mortality rates were completely random from one age to the next—it would be extremely difficult for insurance actuaries to forecast the life expectancy of a particular group of annuitants.

In summary, the mortality rate is the probability that an individual from a fairly homogenous group of insured lives will die during a given year. By placing a large number of similar individuals together in a group, an insurance company can accurately forecast how long it will be making payments to the entire group, even if the behavior of individuals in the group is difficult to predict. The forecast is based on a particular mortality table. The key is to pick the right table.

Q15. How Are Mortality Rates Converted into Survival Probabilities?

The mortality rate gives year-by-year estimates of the age-dependent probability of death for a given group, but for the purposes of pricing and valuing life annuities, the mortality rate must be converted into a survival rate. Technically, survival rates are a set of (declining) numbers that describe the probability of living 1, 10, 20, and even 50 years into the future. And although a 1% mortality rate for someone who is 70 years old obviously implies a 99% probability of surviving to the age of 71, extending those numbers to more advanced ages is messy. Equation 2 describes how to convert mortality rates into long-term survival rates under the assumption that the age-based

l_x, remain the same over time. The left-hand side is obtained ...gether the quantities given by 1 less the mortality rate from ...til the age to which survival is being projected:

$$p(x, i) = \prod_{j=0}^{i-1} \left(1 - q_{x+j}\right). \tag{2}$$

The expression $p(x, i)$ represents the probability that an x-year-old, who is alive, will survive to his $(x + i)$ birthday. So, for example, $p(75, 10)$ denotes the probability a 75-year-old will survive 10 more years to his 85th birthday, and $p(80, 5)$ denotes the probability an 80-year-old will survive 5 more years to her 85th birthday. Naturally, for the same set of underlying mortality rates, the rate for survival from 80 to 85 is greater than the rate for survival from 75 to 85 because in the former, the person is already alive at 80. (The question is, Who is more likely to reach his or her 85th birthday?)

The other expression in Equation 2 should be familiar from Equation 1; q_{x+j} denotes the probability that a $(x + j)$-year-old will die during the next year, before his or her next birthday. For example, q_{65} is the probability that a 65-year-old will die before the 66th birthday.

Thus, whereas Equation 1 defined the mortality rate, Equation 2 shows the probability of staying alive over a given period of time.

Here is a detailed example of how to use Equation 2: Assume that, based on a given mortality table, the probability a 70-year-old will die before his 71st birthday is ($q_{70} = 1.35065\%$); the probability a 71-year-old will die before her 72nd birthday is ($q_{71} = 1.50065\%$); and the probability a 72-year-old will die before his 73rd birthday is ($q_{70} = 1.66765\%$). (Never mind for now where exactly these numbers come from or how they were estimated.) According to Equation 2, the probability that a 70-year-old will survive for 3 more years (i.e., not die before his 71st, 72nd, or 73rd birthday) is the product of the quantities given by 1 minus these three individual rates. Using our notation the answer is $p(70, 3) = 93.777\%$.

Table 6 provides an entire vector of survival probabilities—for a given mortality table—starting from age 70 all the way to the last age at which it is assumed members of the group might still be alive. The mortality rates used in one column of Table 6 are a 50/50 blend of "individual annuitant" mortality rates for males and females observed in 2000; the table is thus often called a "unisex table." The survival probabilities would be slightly higher for females and slightly lower for males.

Notice how the survival probability (in the last column) declines from a value of 98.649%—which is the probability of surviving for 1 year—down to a value of zero by the age of 115. Think of a continuous curve that begins at a value of 1.0 (probability of surviving for one small instant) and then gradually declines toward zero (no one gets out of here alive). This decline is more rapid than exponential

Table 6. From Monthly Mortality Rates to Survival Probabilities as of 2000

| Age | Mortality Rate | | | Survival from Age 70 to End of Year |
	Female	Male	50/50 Blend Unisex	
70	1.0034%	1.6979	1.351%	98.649%
71	1.1117	1.8891	1.500	97.169
72	1.2386	2.0967	1.668	95.549
73	1.3871	2.3209	1.854	93.777
74	1.5592	2.5644	2.062	91.844
75	1.7564	2.8304	2.293	89.737
76	1.9805	3.1220	2.551	87.448
77	2.2328	3.4425	2.838	84.967
78	2.5158	3.7948	3.155	82.286
79	2.8341	4.1812	3.508	79.399
80	3.1933	4.6037	3.899	76.304
81	3.5985	5.0643	4.331	72.999
82	4.0552	5.5651	4.810	69.488
83	4.5690	6.1080	5.339	65.778
84	5.1456	6.6948	5.920	61.884
85	5.7913	7.3275	6.559	57.825
86	6.5119	8.0076	7.260	53.627
87	7.3136	8.7370	8.025	49.323
88	8.1991	9.5169	8.858	44.954
89	9.1577	10.3455	9.752	40.570
90	10.1758	11.2208	10.698	36.230
91	11.2395	12.1402	11.690	31.995
92	12.3349	13.1017	12.718	27.925
93	13.4486	14.1030	13.776	24.079
94	14.5689	15.1422	14.856	20.502
95	15.6846	16.2179	15.951	17.231
96	16.7841	17.3279	17.056	14.292
97	17.8563	18.4706	18.163	11.696
98	18.9604	19.6946	19.328	9.436
99	20.1557	21.0484	20.602	7.492
100	21.5013	22.5806	22.041	5.841
101	23.0565	24.3398	23.698	4.456
102	24.8805	26.3745	25.628	3.314
103	27.0326	28.7334	27.883	2.390
104	29.5719	31.4649	30.518	1.661
105	32.5576	34.6177	33.588	1.103
106	36.0491	38.2403	37.145	0.693
107	40.1064	42.3813	41.243	0.407

(continued)

Table 6. From Monthly Mortality Rates to Survival Probabilities as of 2000 (continued)

| | Mortality Rate | | | |
| | | | 50/50 Blend | Survival from Age 70 to End |
Age	Female	Male	Unisex	of Year
108	44.7860%	47.0893%	45.938%	0.220%
109	50.1498	52.4128	51.281	0.107
110	56.2563	58.4004	57.328	0.046
111	63.1645	65.1007	64.133	0.016
112	70.9338	72.5622	71.748	0.005
113	79.6233	80.8336	80.228	0.001
114	89.2923	89.9633	89.628	0.000
115	100.0000	100.0000	100.000	0.000

Source: Based on data from Society of Actuaries.

but not as fast as linear. The probability of a 70-year-old surviving to age 80 is about 76%; the probability of that person surviving to 85 is approximately 58%; finally, the probability of the person surviving to 100 is a bit less than 6%. Stated differently, the mortality table indicates that 76% of a large group of 70-year-olds (in the referenced group) will survive to age 80, that 58% of them will survive to age 85, and that 6% of them will survive to age 100. Of course, these rates are all projections for future mortality based on past trends, recent improvements, and so on. As with trying to predict the odds of the stock market going up or down in any given year or decade, all we have is historical data.

The underlying mortality table reflects the experience of the insurance industry with annuitants—that is, retirees who actually purchase annuities. These people tend to be healthier than population averages, experience lower mortality rates, and, therefore, live longer. U.S. Social Security mortality tables reflect a wider (and less healthy) group of individuals. Of course, regardless of what mortality rates are used in the right-hand side of Equation 2, the corresponding survival probabilities, given those rates, are obtained by using that equation.

The probability of surviving any given number of years depends critically on the age on which the individual life is being *conditioned*. The probability of surviving to age 90, for example, depends on the current age (as well as gender, health, etc.). Someone who is 89 years old has a greater chance of making it to age 90 than someone who is only 85 years old. This mathematical fact is embedded in the logic of Equation 2. The probability of surviving to age 90 if you are 89 is $(1 - q_{89})$, but the probability of surviving to age 90 if you are

85 is $(1 - q_{85})(1 - q_{86})(1 - q_{87})(1 - q_{88})(1 - q_{89})$, a smaller number. It is smaller because in this case, we are multiplying the quantity $(1 - q_{89})$, which is present in both cases, by other numbers that are all smaller than 1.0.

To conclude, the "fundamental particle" used in pricing and valuing any life annuity is the underlying mortality rate, presented in a mortality rate table, which is sometimes referred to as the "mortality basis." There are many different types of mortality tables, and like snowflakes, no two are exactly alike. There are mortality tables for healthy and wealthy females and mortality tables for unhealthy, unwealthy males. There are mortality tables for entire populations, and there are mortality tables for small groups of retired annuitants. Whatever population the table represents, the rates in the table can be used to create a unique set of survival probabilities based on Equation 2. Moreover, it is easy to work backward and recover or extract mortality rates from survival probabilities. In fact, as an exercise, you might try to recover the second-to-last column in Table 6 from the survival probabilities.

Finally, anytime someone mentions or displays a survival probability curve—whether or not it is within the context of life annuity pricing—you should ask yourself, What was the underlying mortality table on which these survival rates were based?

Q16. What Is the Benjamin Gompertz Law of Mortality?

The age-dependent mortality rates displayed in the first two columns of Table 6 might seem arbitrary at first, but they have a clear underlying pattern. The mortality rates not only increase with age, but they also actually increase by almost the same percentage amount every year. In other words, if the mortality rate was $q\%$ at age y, then it was $q(1 + z\%)$ in year $(y + 1)$, then $q(1 + z\%)^2$ in year $(y + 2)$, $q(1 + z\%)^3$ in year $(y + 3)$, and so on. Human mortality rates—regardless of the particular mortality table you select—are for the most part an exponentially increasing function of age. So, if you compute the logarithms of the annual mortality rates, they can be approximated nicely by a straight line and determined by (1) a slope parameter and (2) an intercept parameter. Think of it as a law of biology. At the beginning of the 21st century, z is approximately 9%, so in any given population, approximately 9% more individuals of a certain age will die this year compared with last year. If 100,000 Americans who are 65 years old died in 2012; therefore, the estimate is that 109,000 Americans who are 66 years old will die in 2013. Notice the age dependency and the link to the previous year.

Of course, I did not stumble on this law, nor is it a fluke of the data. This biological observation was first made by the British demographer and actuary Benjamin Gompertz (1779–1865), and it is today known as the "Gompertz law of mortality." His groundbreaking research on human mortality modeling was first published in 1825 in *Philosophical Transactions of the Royal Society*; it is one of the foundational papers in the field of actuarial science and demographics.

The reason this observation is more than actuarial trivia is that it gives us a powerful analytical tool to compute survival probabilities to any age as a function of only two basic parameters—the slope and intercept in the previously mentioned straight line. This tool both simplifies the computational requirements and provides intuition for the annuity pricing formulas (yet to come).[21]

The exact derivation is beyond the scope of this book, but the concise formula for the survival probability—from any age to any age—under the Gompertz law of mortality can be written as follows:

$$\ln\left[\,p\left(x,t\right)\right] = \left(1 - e^{t/b}\right)e^{\left(\frac{x-m}{b}\right)}, \tag{3}$$

where t denotes the survival period, x denotes the current age of the individual, and the parameters (m, b) denote, respectively, the modal age at death and the dispersion coefficient of the age at death, both in years. These parameters are described in the following material, but a simple way to understand them is to think of a baby who is born today with the most likely age at which he or she will die being, for example, $m = 80$ and the (approximate) standard deviation around that age being, for example, $b = 10$. The survival probability itself—which is the main quantity of interest—is obtained by taking the exponent of the right-hand side of Equation 3.

Here is a detailed example: Assume that you are currently 50 years old and would like to estimate the probability you will live (at least) to the age of 90, which is 40 more years. According to the Gompertz law of mortality, this probability depends on two parameters—m, the modal age at death (roughly speaking, the age to which you can expect to live) and b, the dispersion coefficient of m. Thus, these two numbers can loosely be thought of as the mean and standard deviation of the length of your lifetime, which is obviously a random variable.

Keep in mind that the parameters (m, b) are characteristics of a population of a group of people, so $m = 80$ means that a member of the population can expect at the time of birth to live to (about) 80. The remaining life expectancy for an individual at age x is a different concept, given by the conditional probability, which will be higher than $(m - x)$.

---

[21]In the early 21st century, with cheap and vast computational power available, actuaries tend to use actual (discrete) mortality tables, rather than closed-form analytic laws, to price and value life annuities. But these sorts of rules and laws were a godsend when calculations had to be done by hand. More importantly, and as any financial economist will attest, being able to reduce the price of a capital asset down to a few critical parameters is prized for its own sake.

Remember that if $T(x)$ represents the random number of years you will live from age x onward—that is, the remaining lifetime random variable—then, for example, the expectation $E[T(65)] > E[T(45)] - 20$. So, be careful to distinguish between expectations at age zero and conditional expectations at any higher age.[22]

Technically, the modal age at death is the age at which you are most likely to die. It is actually a few years higher than the median (the age at which 50% of people your age will have died and 50% will still be alive). The reason is the skewness of the distribution. In simple terms, if the modal age at death is $m = 80$ years and the dispersion value is $b = 11$ years, then according to Equation 3, the survival probability to age 90 is 8.9%, which can also be expressed as a 91.1% probability of dying prior to age 90. In contrast, with a higher modal age at death, $m = 92$ (instead of $m = 80$) years in Equation 3, the survival probability to age 90 increases to 44.4%. Note how the extra 12 years of life (in the modal sense) add 35.5 percentage points to the survival probability. In fact, if you "believe" that your modal age at death is indeed $m = 92$ years, then, according to Equation 3, the probability of surviving to age 95 (from age 50) is 27.5% and the probability of surviving to age 100 and becoming a centenarian is 12.9%. That probability is obviously optimistic, but thus says the Gompertz law of mortality when $m = 92$ and $b = 11$. The problem is that the inputs are almost certainly unrealistic.

Figure 3 provides a graphical indication of how the survival probabilities under the Gompertz law of mortality are affected by the modal age at death, m. In all four cases, the dispersion coefficient, b, is taken to be 11 years, but the modal age at death ranges from $m = 80$ to $m = 92$. Notice how all four curves start off at a value of 100% but decline toward zero. By the age of 110, all four curves are close to zero. The difference between the individual curves is the rate at which the probabilities decline toward zero. The curve with the lowest m value declines at the fastest pace. From a qualitative perspective, the curves look similar to the survival values displayed in the last column of Table 6. In fact, I leave as an exercise for the reader to use Excel and locate the best fitting parameters (m, b) that would minimize the distance between the survival curve defined by Figure 3 and the numbers displayed in Table 6.

The question is, of course, which parameters to use in practice when trying to forecast survival probabilities and/or trying to price life annuities. As you can plainly see, changing the modal age at death by only a few years can have a dramatic effect on the probabilities. The issue is analogous to using the lognormal distribution to approximate long-term portfolio returns. The analytics

---

[22]That is, m is unconditional, as opposed to a conditional moment of a random variable. Another way to think of m and b is in purely geometric terms as the two degrees of freedom embedded within slope and intercept of the logarithm of the mortality rate.

Figure 3.   Analytic Law of Mortality: Gompertz Survival Probabilities for Various Modal Values, *m*, at Death

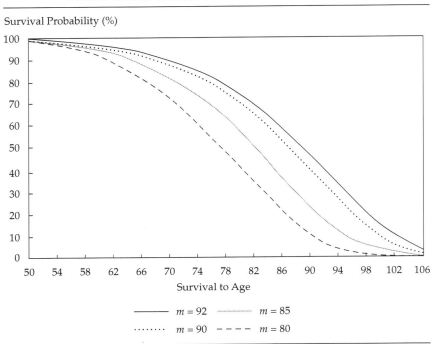

Note: The dispersion coefficient, *b*, is 11 years.

are well understood, but the parameters are debatable. Should you assume an expected return of 4% from stocks or closer to 8%? The same issues apply when it comes to mortality and longevity modeling under any parametric law of mortality. And it is in this area that historical data and current mortality rates are used to calibrate such a model. The good news is that the mortality models, such as the Gompertz law (or its extension, the Makeham law), tend to "fit" the ages around retirement remarkably well. Although I do not want to get caught up in the actuarial minutiae and demographic details, the Gompertz law of mortality has withstood the test of time.

In summary, there are two ways of working with (and thinking about) retirement survival probabilities, which are part of the DNA of annuity pricing. The first approach is to start with a mortality table that is applicable to a given population group and then compute (using Equation 2) the relevant survival rates. This approach can get messy, is computationally cumbersome, and is not intuitive, but it is actually the route preferred by insurance actuaries who perform these calculations. The second—more elegant and certainly easier—approach is to "select" the best fitting modal, *m*, and dispersion, *b*, values for the population or individual in question—based on a given mortality table or population mortality—and then use Equation 3 to compute the survival probabilities. The numbers are close because of the underlying Gompertz law of mortality.

Fortunately, for all intents and purposes, the Gompertz approximation is good when it comes to pricing life annuities at retirement, which is the subject of the next section's formula.

Q17. Valuation: What Is the Gompertz Annuity Pricing Model?

What you pay for a life annuity—or the amount of income you can expect for a given premium deposit—is determined in a competitive market based on the interaction of numerous insurance companies. So, although the actual price you pay is partially determined by the forces of supply and demand, a strict mathematical relationship links mortality expectations and interest rates to observed prices. This idea is akin to the concept of arbitrage in securities markets, in which the prices you pay for securities with similar characteristics should not vary much from one another.

The most basic pricing formula (or asset pricing equation) for a life annuity—and probably the most important formula in this book—can be expressed as follows:

$$a(x,g,R) = \sum_{i=1}^{g} \frac{1}{(1+R)^i} + \sum_{i=g+1}^{\omega-x} \frac{p(x,i)}{(1+R)^i}. \tag{4}$$

The expression $a(x, g, R)$ denotes the upfront "cost" of \$1 per year for life, starting at the age of x, guaranteed for g periods, given annual nominal interest rate R. On the right-hand side, you see two terms: the guaranteed portion and the life-contingent portion. In the life-contingent portion, which is the rightmost term, the ratios of the survival probability, $p(x, i)$, and the interest rate factor, $(1 + R)^i$, are added up until the end of the mortality table. Technically, the sum terminates at the age of ω (omega), which denotes the oldest possible age attainable.

Equation 4 differs from the standard present value formula by having the survival-contingent probability instead of the standard \$1 in the numerator of the summation. So, you can think of Equation 4 as the present value factor of \$1 of income to be received for as long as you are alive. For example, if you are 70 years old and the probability of surviving for 1 year is 97%, for 2 years is 95%, and for 3 years is 92%, then the first three terms of the life-contingent present value embedded in Equation 4 are $[0.97/(1.05)^1] + [0.95/(1.05)^2] + [0.92/(10.05)^3]$, with the remaining terms declining in importance until the final numerator is zero.

To be precise, you can use any survival probability vector of numbers in the numerator of Equation 4 and add up the terms to arrive at $a(x, g, R)$. Yet, a closed-form expression for the life annuity factor $a(x, g, R)$ can be obtained when mortality is assumed to obey the Gompertz law and payments occur in continuous time. The process involves the incomplete gamma function, $\Gamma(A, B)$. The mathematics of this process go well beyond this book, but for a pure life annuity with no PC, the model price is found with the Gompertz annuity pricing model (GAPM):

$$a(x,g,r) = \frac{\left(1-e^{-rg}\right)}{r} + \frac{b\Gamma\{-rb, \exp[(x-m+g)/b]\}}{\exp\{[m-x]r - \exp[(x-m)/b]\}},\qquad (5)$$

where r denotes the continuously compounded interest rate, or $r = \ln(1 + R)$. This equation is GAPM for a life annuity that is guaranteed for g years (see Chapter 6 of Milevsky 2006 for a derivation). In contrast to many other asset pricing models, the GAPM fits market prices quite well.

Table 7 displays the actual (market) payouts available from U.S. life annuities in late August 2012—based on the average of the best five company quotes—and compares them with outputs from the GAPM. The model parameters are ($m = 89.81$, $b = 11.61$) for males and ($m = 92.06$, $b = 11.1$) for females. The interest rate used in Equation 4 is $R = 2.88\%$ for both males and females. For comparison purposes, this interest rate was approximately 0.60% lower than the 30-year fixed-rate mortgage at the time and approximately 0.30% higher than the 30-year T-bond yield. The three model parameters (m, b, R) required to fit market prices were selected by use of a nonlinear procedure minimizing the squared distance between the 30 payouts in the pricing matrix.

Note that the model and market prices (for monthly income) are within $15 of each other. For example, if you plug the values of $m = 89.81$ and $b = 11.61$ into Equation 3 for survival rates and then plug those rates into annuity pricing Equation 4 with a constant interest rate of $R = 2.88\%$, the resulting annuity factor at the age of $x = 65$ is (approximately) $15.461 per dollar of lifetime income. So, if you spend $100,000 on such a life annuity, you will be entitled to $6,468 (100,000/15.461) per year, which is $539 per month. This model value is a mere $7 more (in terms of monthly income) than what was offered by the (average) insurance company in August 2012.

To conclude, no formula in finance (even the Black–Scholes option pricing formula) can provide a perfect fit to the observed price of a financial asset traded in the market, but the "life annuity factor" described by Equation 4—and the GAPM of Equation 5—provides a reasonably good fit to quotes offered by insurance companies. For those in need of a quick number, Equation 4 is the key.

Table 7.   Market Prices vs. GAPM: Life Annuity Payouts per $100,000 Premium, August 2012

Age	0-Year PC	5-Year PC	10-Year PC	15-Year PC	20-Year PC
A. Males					
55	Market = $431	Market = $430	Market = $427	Market = $422	Market = $414
	Model = $431	Model = $430	Model = $426	Model = $419	Model = $409
60	Market = $475	Market = $473	Market = $468	Market = $459	Market = $443
	Model = $478	Model = $475	Model = $468	Model = $456	Model = $438
65	Market = $532	Market = $529	Market = $519	Market = $499	Market = $470
	Model = $539	Model = $534	Model = $520	Model = $498	Model = $469
70	Market = $613	Market = $606	Market = $585	Market = $544	Market = $497
	Model = $620	Model = $611	Model = $585	Model = $545	Model = $498
75	Market = $729	Market = $713	Market = $664	Market = $589	Market = $516
	Model = $730	Model = $712	Model = $661	Model = $592	Model = $522
80	Market = $895	Market = $865	Market = $749	Market = $623	Market = $524
	Model = $882	Model = $842	Model = $744	Model = $633	Model = $537
B. Females					
55	Market = $416	Market = $416	Market = $414	Market = $409	Market = $403
	Model = $416	Model = $415	Model = $412	Model = $407	Model = $399
60	Market = $456	Market = $455	Market = $451	Market = $443	Market = $432
	Model = $457	Model = $456	Model = $451	Model = $442	Model = $428
65	Market = $507	Market = $505	Market = $497	Market = $482	Market = $461
	Model = $513	Model = $509	Model = $499	Model = $483	Model = $460
70	Market = $578	Market = $574	Market = $557	Market = $527	Market = $491
	Model = $586	Model = $579	Model = $560	Model = $529	Model = $491
75	Market = $686	Market = $674	Market = $635	Market = $579	Market = $513
	Model = $685	Model = $672	Model = $633	Model = $578	Model = $518
80	Market = $838	Market = $809	Market = $724	Market = $617	Market = $523
	Model = $823	Model = $793	Model = $717	Model = $623	Model = $536

Notes: "Market" price is the average of actual market quotes for males or females. "Model" price is the output of the GAPM.
Source: QWeMA Group analysis based on data from Cannex Financial.

Q18. What Are the Duration and Interest Rate Sensitivity of a Life Annuity?

A life annuity is a type of fixed-income product—one in which the coupons are higher than those of government or corporate bonds, partly because of the annuity's illiquidity. This unique and personal longevity-linked bond is subject to default (i.e., your death), at which point only a small fraction of the original investment will be recovered by creditors (i.e., your heirs). Continuing with the "defaultable bond" analogy, we can say that the life annuity value is sensitive to mortality rates and interest rates. And as with any traded bond, its price (or value) will fluctuate on the basis of changes in interest rates. So, although a life annuity paying $1,000 a month cannot be (easily) traded after it has been purchased—nor does it really have a market value in the conventional trading sense—it does have an ongoing "theoretical" value, which declines as you age. That is, the closer you are to death, the less the same $1,000 monthly income is worth and the less you should have to pay for it. Over short periods of time, however, interest rate changes are what drive life annuity price changes, an observation that brings us to the topic of duration.

The duration of a life annuity is defined as the derivative of the annuity factor with respect to changes in the valuation rate, scaled by the (negative) annuity factor itself. Formally, it is expressed as follows:

$$D(x,g,R) = \frac{-\partial a(x,g,R)/\partial R}{a(x,g,R)} = \frac{-1}{a(x,g,R)} \sum_{i=1}^{\omega-x} i\,\bar{p}(x,i)(1+R)^{-(i+1)}. \tag{6}$$

Equation 6 includes the usual variables, but I have modified the expression for the survival probability, $\bar{p}(x,i)$, to embed guarantee period g. So, the survival probability is $p(x,i|g) = 1$ as long as $i \leq g$ and then jumps to $\bar{p}(x,i) = p(x,i)$ when $i > g$. Also, time variable g can be measured in days, weeks, months, or years. This shorthand notation allows me to avoid breaking the summation into two distinct portions.

Here is what matters: The greater the life annuity's duration, $D(x,g,R)$, the more sensitive it is to changes in interest rates. Moreover, as is similar to the duration for any conventional bond, we can approximate the percentage change in the value of a life annuity by multiplying the (negative) duration by the relevant change in interest rates. This result can be expressed as follows:

$$\frac{a(x,g,R+\Delta R) - a(x,g,R)}{a(x,g,R)} = \frac{\Delta a(x,g,R)}{a(x,g,R)} \approx -D(x,g,R)\Delta R. \tag{7}$$

I will provide numerical examples in a moment, but note that Equations 6 and 7 are versatile and can be used in many different ways. The survival probabilities can be (1) taken from a mortality table, (2) assumed on the basis of a given analytical law of mortality, or (3) implied from actual life annuity prices. I will provide more on this subject later.

Table 8 provides values for the duration of a life annuity at various ages and assuming different PC guarantees under the GAPM. Notice how duration uniformly declines with age but does not necessarily change in a predictable manner when the guarantee period is increased. Indeed, the derivative of the duration with respect to the guaranteed period is indeterminate, but the derivative with respect to age is negative.

Here is how to understand the numbers in Table 8. Take, for example, a male retiring at the age of 65 and buying a life annuity with a 10-year PC. The annuity factor under the GAPM, based on Equation 5, is $11.92 per dollar of lifetime annual income. So, a $100,000 premium would translate into $8,389 (100,000/11.92) in annual income, $700 in monthly income, or $161 in weekly income. These model value payout rates are slightly higher than the rates in the summer of 2012.

Table 8. Theoretical Duration of Life Annuity: Males vs. Females
(duration in years)

Age	0-Year PC	5-Year PC	10-Year PC	15-Year PC	20-Year PC
Age 55	M = 11.03	M = 11.00	M = 10.97	M = 11.00	M = 11.14
	F = 11.91	F = 11.90	F = 11.88	F = 11.89	F = 11.95
Age 60	M = 10.02	M = 9.98	M = 9.94	M = 10.02	M = 10.28
	F = 10.90	F = 10.88	F = 10.86	F = 10.88	F = 11.01
Age 65	M = 8.96	M = 8.90	M = 8.87	M = 9.03	M = 9.50
	F = 9.82	F = 9.78	F = 9.76	F = 9.83	F = 10.09
Age 70	M = 7.87	M = 7.78	M = 7.78	M = 8.12	M = 8.88
	F = 8.66	F = 8.61	F = 8.59	F = 8.77	F = 9.26
Age 75	M = 6.76	M = 6.64	M = 6.73	M = 7.37	M = 8.47
	F = 7.47	F = 7.39	F = 7.41	F = 7.81	F = 8.66
Age 80	M = 5.67	M = 5.52	M = 5.82	M = 6.85	M = 8.28
	F = 6.26	F = 6.15	F = 6.30	F = 7.07	F = 8.33

Note: In the GAPM, under a constant 5.46% interest rate, with mortality parameters of ($m = 88.15$, $b = 10.50$) for males and ($m = 92.63$, $b = 8.78$) for females.
Source: Based on data from Charupat, Kamstra, and Milevsky (2012).

Now, consider the duration numbers. If the underlying interest rate were to suddenly increase by 0.50% (i.e., 50 bps), the same $700 monthly income would cost less than $100,000. In fact, a $100,000 premium would lead to more lifetime income because pricing interest rates have increased. The question is, By how much would the cost of the $700 monthly income decline? The answer lies in the duration of the annuity factor, which from Table 8 is $D(65, 10, 5.46\%) = 8.87$ years for a 65-year-old male with a 10-year PC. So, finally, according to Equation 7, the annuity factor would decline by 4.435% ([8.87][0.005] = 0.04435). The same life annuity (stream of income) would cost $95,565 ($100,000[1 − 0.04435]) instead of $100,000.

Notice, again, how the duration at advanced ages is much lower than for younger ages—for example, 11 years at age 55 versus 6 years at age 80—which implies a much lower sensitivity to changes in interest rates as a person ages. Practically speaking, retirees in their late 70s and early 80s who are interested in acquiring a life annuity but are "waiting for interest rates to improve" might be surprised to learn that interest rates increasing by a percentage or two will not make much difference in their income. In a person's 70s and early 80s, mortality rates are what drive payouts.

In conclusion, the duration number provides a quick-and-easy indication of the sensitivity of a life annuity's value to a change in interest rates. So, if you want to forecast how much more income you might get—for a given premium—if rates increased by a few percentage points, duration is the closest you will get to a crystal ball.

Of course, whether *actual* annuity prices will adjust to *actual* changes in interest rates based on these duration values is an empirical question for another book.

Q19. What Is the Money's Worth Ratio of a Life Annuity?

Up to this point, I have been careless with such terms as "market value," "model price," and "theoretical cost" of a life annuity. As you might recall, I displayed some market prices and some mathematically contrived values, and I then discussed various combinations of the two. To add to the confusion, I have also been vague about the exact mortality rates—or mortality parameters—that should be used in annuity pricing models. This approach has been deliberate, but in this section, I would like to take the opportunity to clean up terminology and be more precise about the links between (1) model values and (2) the market price of a life annuity. And although you might expect the two numbers to be close to each other—and the GAPM provides values that are within a few dollars of market prices—in this section, I will formally compare these two numbers.

The metric that connects the two is called the "money's worth ratio" (MWR). Formally, it is defined as follows:

$$\text{MWR} = \frac{\text{Model value}}{\text{Market price}}.$$

(8)

The numerator in Equation 8 is the result of a formal mathematical relationship mapping mortality, interest rates, and transaction costs into a single output number. The denominator is the actual price paid by the purchaser of a life annuity, or at least the number quoted for the annuity.

If we assume that model values are close to market prices, then the MWR in Equation 8 should be in the vicinity of 1.0. A higher ratio—numerator greater than denominator—obviously implies a better deal for consumers. And although the words "money's worth" might emit a strong aura of economic efficiency and fairness, remember that the numerator involves a *model with particular assumptions* and the denominator is a *snapshot of a price* at a given point in time. Both quantities are subject to biases, which is something I will discuss later.

Notwithstanding some of these concerns, the MWR has become *the* metric used to measure, compare, and contrast the efficiency of annuity markets around the world. To my knowledge, at least three dozen research articles have been published in the past two decades—all cited in the bibliography—that have examined the MWR in countries from Singapore to Chile. Much of this work has been conducted under the auspices of the International Monetary Fund (IMF). Countries and markets with high MWR (MWR > 1.0) are deemed to provide good value for consumers, whereas countries where MWR < 1 are classified as providing less value.

Table 9 provides a limited sample of these studies from various English-speaking countries. Notice how most numbers are less than 1.0, except for Canada, which is a curious matter, but we can only speculate as to the reasons.

Table 9. MWR in Various Annuity Markets

Country	Annuitant Mortality Rate		Population Mortality Rate	
	Male	Female	Male	Female
United States	0.927	0.927	0.814	0.852
Canada	1.17	1.06	0.965	0.937
United Kingdom	0.96–0.98	0.94–0.93	0.90–0.86	0.90–0.85
Australia	0.986	0.970	0.914	0.910

Note: A number of studies have measured MWR in the United Kingdom; the numbers here are the range reported.
Source: Based on data from Nielson (2012).

The MWR values are higher when annuitant mortality rates are used in the numerator of Equation 8 than when population mortality rates are used. Remember that annuitant mortality implies a much higher survival probability than population mortality. This contrast gets to the heart of the issue: The MWR is about comparing a model price with a market price. Naturally, if the model price assumes that people are going to live (much) longer, then the numerator will be greater; hence, the MWR, as calculated, will be higher. (I will soon discuss why the MWR may not measure true "money's worth.")

Here is an example of how the MWR is computed: Start with a $100,000 annuity premium (investment) and assume that it would generate $500 per month for life for a 65-year-old male with a 15-year PC. This number would be an average quote from the relevant insurance companies. The MWR metric is usually applied to a market as opposed to an individual company, so the denominator of Equation 8 would be the $100,000 premium.

Moving on to the numerator: The $500 per month, or $6,000 per year, of lifetime income is multiplied by the annuity factor pricing model—the GAPM described previously with a given assumption for (1) mortality rates and (2) interest rates. The mortality rates could be average population rates or healthier annuitant rates. Similarly, the interest rate could be a fixed number or an entire term structure of rates. In fact, these rates could be risk-free government rates or risky corporate rates. Once all these assumptions (i.e., modeling decisions) have been made, the resulting annuity factor is multiplied by the $6,000 income and, finally, compared with the $100,000 premium. The ratio of these two numbers is the MWR. Obviously, very different MWR values can be obtained depending on the exact assumptions made for the annuity pricing model.

Although the MWR is widely used by researchers, people should keep in mind a number of issues or concerns when interpreting results of such studies. First, insurance companies with low credit ratings (which are likely to offer more on life annuities) will report higher MWR values. Second, these numbers tend to be snapshots in time. Third, they are driven by model and pricing assumptions involving both mortality and interest rate expectations over long periods of time.

When compared with asset pricing models in financial economics, annuity pricing models produce remarkably better fits with market prices. In fact, using the GAPM, for example, you can fit market payouts to within a few dollars, as displayed in Table 7. Nevertheless, this section is not meant to boast about goodness of fit but, rather, to remind readers how critical mortality assumptions are when pricing and valuing life annuities. Depending on your mortality model, you might get MWR values that exceed unity by as much as 10% or fall short of unity by as much as 20%. What this means from a purely economic point of view should be clear. A life annuity is worth (much) less to you personally if you are in average health (that is, health typical of the overall population) than if you are in excellent (annuitant) health.

Finally, I recommend, in jest, that if you do have the choice, you should buy your annuity in the country with the highest MWR.

Q20. Can You Afford to Wait? Introducing the Implied Longevity Yield

Life annuities yield more income than non-mortality-linked fixed-income instruments because the annuities' benefits accrue only to the exclusive club of survivors. In this section, I will present a new and intuitive method for understanding the magnitude of these benefits. The metric is called the "implied longevity yield" (ILY) and is yet another way to think about mortality credits.[23]

To understand the context of the ILY metric, think in terms of the natural option everyone has—and many use—to simply delay annuitization. As most procrastinators would argue, why do something today if you can wait until tomorrow, next week, or even next year? What is the urgency of now? The same question might apply to buying a life annuity. It is costly. It is irreversible. What's the rush? Bear with me for a moment and imagine the following situation. You are 65 years old and have $100,000 available to finance your retirement spending. So (perhaps after reading this book), you are thinking of annuitizing. Should you wait?

Assume that if you were to annuitize today, you would receive $517 in monthly income (with zero PC), which is $6,204 of yearly income, for life. This outcome can also be expressed as a cash yield of 6.2% for life, which obviously includes the return of principal. Now, this embedded return of principal makes it difficult to directly compare the 6.2% with, say, a 10-year government bond yielding a coupon of (only) 2.4% on the same day as the annuity quote. Alas, the 3.8% difference between the two numbers overstates the benefit from the life annuity because of the blended mixture of interest and principal. So, how do you (properly) compare the two? What is the actual spread over, say, U.S. Treasury rates, which results from joining a longevity pool?

Following on the idea of procrastination, imagine that instead of buying the $517 monthly annuity now, you decide to (1) wait for 10 years, (2) systematically withdraw the $517 from an investment portfolio in the meantime, and then (3) try to purchase the same $517 life annuity at age 75. This approach is called "self-annuitization," and although forecasting how much the identical $517 monthly annuity might cost in 10 years' time is difficult, a good proxy is available—namely, today's price. Suppose that on the same day as the

---

[23]The ILY is now a registered trademark of Cannex Financial Exchanges. More information on the algorithm behind the ILY can be found in Milevsky (2005b).

quote for the $100,000 cash policy, a 75-year-old is quoted $704 in monthly income for life—$8,452 in annual income and a life annuity yield of 8.45%. The higher payout is caused by the shorter remaining life expectancy of this person than you, higher mortality rate, and other factors. The bottom line is that if you at 65 decide to wait 10 years and purchase the $517 annuity at age 75 (and assuming prices remain exactly the same), you will need roughly $73,400 ($6,204/0.0845) in 10 years. In the meantime, you have to be careful not to spend more than $26,600 in principal.

So, to beat the annuity benefit of buying as a 65-year-old, you would have to generate enough interest on the $100,000 that you would have $73,400 left over at the end of 10 years with which to buy the life annuity while withdrawing a $517 monthly income in the meantime.

Once the problem is posed in this manner, the answer boils down to a basic problem in finance. It can be expressed as an internal rate of return (IRR). Formally, the ILY is defined as

$$ \text{ILY} = \text{IRR}\left[t, a(x), \frac{a(x+t)}{a(x)} \right]. \tag{9}$$

The symbol IRR(T, A, B), where T is the first argument, A is the second argument, and B is the third argument, is shorthand notation for the IRR, where the cash flow, A, is paid up front, then $1 is received annually for T years, and then a final cash flow amounting to B dollars is received at the end of T years.[24]

Table 10 displays this example, with the breakeven amount (or IRR) in tabular form. It also provides the same analysis for a 65-year-old female. The numbers are interpreted this way: A 65-year-old male would have to earn at least 4.12% (every year) between the ages of 65 and 75 to be able to purchase the exact same life annuity stream at age 75, *assuming annuity prices remained the same*. This number is 2.43 percentage points greater than the risk-free U.S. government bond listed on the same day on which the annuity quotes were obtained. Therefore, joining the mortality pool between the age of 65 and 75 will yield an extra 2.43 percentage points above the safest asset you could have purchased. If this does not seem like enough to you, then perhaps you should wait to annuitize. The point is to convert the payout from the annuity into a yield number that you can think of as a target to beat.

Note that for females, the ILY is lower than for males. The cause is the mortality credits; that is, the number of people dying between ages 65 and 75 is lower for females, so the subsidy is also lower. Similarly, if the life annuity you purchase at age 65 contains guarantee periods, refunds, and joint-life options and if you receive less than $517 per month (for males) or $485 (for females), the ILY value

---

[24]For those readers who wish to express Equation 9 in Excel, it is *RATE*(T,1,–A,B,0,*guess*).

Table 10.   The Implied Longevity Yield

	Male	Female
A. Monthly income on $100,000 for a 65-year-old who annuitizes	$517.00	$485.00
B. Needed if person wants to purchase the same income stream as a 75-year-old	$73,400	$74,500
C. Annualized 10-year return required on $100,000 to generate monthly income in row A and have enough left over to purchase row B	4.12%	3.77%
D. Yield on 10-year U.S. government bond (November 2012)	1.69%	1.69%
E. Spread on bond yield	2.43%	2.08%

Notes: Payouts assume zero guarantee period. Average of 17 quoting companies as of 22 November 2012.

will be lower. In fact, many retirees purchase life annuities or annuitize a portion of their nest eggs but add on various guarantees, which then greatly reduce and water down the mortality credits. In many cases, the ILY values are little above government bond yields. Once again, you are not really buying much of a life annuity if the ILY is close to what you could get from the safest investment possible.

To conclude, even if you have no intention of annuitizing today (or in the future), the ILY provides an alternative perspective on the threshold, or benchmark investment return, required to beat the life annuity.

Q21. What Is the Lifetime Ruin Probability from Self-Annuitizing?

In the previous section, I dealt with the return required to induce an investor to delay annuitization. I described the breakeven rate known as the "implied longevity yield" that you would have to earn, while waiting to annuitize, to be able to purchase the same annuity stream at some fixed date in the future. In this section, I continue this theme and address a related question: What if you decide to forgo annuitization entirely? What is the probability you can maintain a given withdrawal rate and standard of living while you are still alive? Inspired by the insurance literature, this question has become known as the "lifetime ruin probability" (LRP). It is the probability that your *biological* lifetime will be longer than the *financial* lifetime of your portfolio.

Technically, the formula can be expressed as a present value:

$$
LRP(w,x,\mu,\sigma) = Pr\left[\sum_{t=1}^{\omega-x} \frac{p(x,t)}{\prod_{j=1}^{t}(1+R_j)} > w \right],
\tag{10}
$$

where the portfolio spending rate is $1/w$ (which is the inverse of initial wealth w on the right-hand side), x is the initial age of the retiree, $p(x, t)$ is the survival probability curve, ω is the maximum age, and R_j is the realized portfolio return in period j. The random variable R_j is a function of the portfolio's asset allocation and is summarized by the return–risk pair of mean and standard deviation (μ, σ) in the LRP. For example, LRP(1/0.05, 65, 0.06, 0.20) denotes the lifetime ruin probability under an assumed spending rate of 5% (i.e., \$5 is spent annually for every \$100 of initial principal) for someone aged 65 investing in a portfolio that is expected to earn 6% with a standard deviation of 20%. The LRP for someone who is trying to replicate the payout from a life annuity would, therefore, be denoted by LRP[$a(x, R)$ x, μ, σ].

The intuition behind Equation 10 is as follows: Assume for the moment that $R_j = R$ is constant. The left-hand term inside the square bracket is the present value of a life annuity cash flow (that is, the annuity factor) because the product $\Pi_{j=1}^{t}(1 + R_i)$ in the denominator collapses to $(1 + R)^t$. The entire expression is the annuity factor. And if the annuity factor is greater than the initial sum of money, w, available to finance spending, the individual is ruined. Generally, when R_j is random, we can only talk about the *probability* that the present value is greater than w, which is what Equation 10 is trying to capture. So, Equation 10 is not an explicit formula. It describes an algorithm.

The LRP value displayed in Equation 10 can be computed in a number of ways. A relatively easy methodology is to simulate a vector of R_j portfolio returns and assume a particular mortality table, $p(x, t)$, then count the number of scenarios in which the mortality-weighted present value is greater than w. This is the Monte Carlo approach to retirement income simulations. Another (more accurate, in my opinion) approach is to analytically represent the LRP as a solution to a partial differential equation and then use numerical schemes to quickly and efficiently solve for the LRP. Although the exact methodology is beyond the scope of this book, in the numerical examples that follow, I will display results on the basis of this approach.[25]

Table 11 provides some examples, in which the reader can see the impact of spending rates and asset allocation on the LRP. Remember that the retiree is trying to replicate the cash flow from a life annuity until the account itself goes broke and runs out of money.

For example, imagine a 65-year-old retiree with \$1,000,000 in investable assets who does not want to purchase a life annuity and, instead, would like to withdraw \$60,000 per year in inflation-adjusted terms from an investment

---

[25]I used an Excel add-in created by the QWeMA Group, which computes a continuous-time version of the LRP by solving the relevant partial differential equation. For more information, visit www.qwema.ca, see the references in Milevsky (2012), or use the approximation in Milevsky and Robinson (2005).

Table 11.   LRP of Self-Annuitization at Age 65

Spending Rate	100% Risky Stocks; 0% Safe Cash	80% Risky Stocks; 20% Safe Cash	60% Risky Stocks; 40% Safe Cash	40% Risky Stocks; 60% Safe Cash	20% Risky Stocks; 80% Safe Cash
2.0%	3.07%	1.41%	0.44%	0.06%	0.00%
2.5	5.71	3.27	1.49	0.43	0.05
3.0	9.14	6.13	3.64	1.78	0.72
3.5	13.23	9.98	7.15	4.94	3.99
4.0	17.81	14.67	12.03	10.38	11.60
4.5	22.70	19.98	18.05	17.86	22.56
5.0	27.75	25.69	24.83	26.61	34.22
5.5	32.83	31.56	31.94	35.65	44.66
6.0	37.82	37.40	39.00	44.23	53.22
6.5	42.66	43.05	45.71	51.86	60.00
7.0	47.26	48.40	51.90	58.38	65.35

portfolio. The $60,000 (inflating) withdrawals will be made from interest, dividends, and principal, if needed. Assume that the portfolio is invested 80% in stocks—with an expected return of 6% and volatility of 20%—and the remaining 20% is in cash yielding 1.5%. All returns are in inflation-adjusted terms. In this case, the arithmetic mean return of the portfolio is $\mu = 5.10\%$ and the volatility is $\sigma = 16\%$. The spending rate of 6% is equivalent to $w = 1/0.06 = \$16.666$ per dollar of spending.

According to Table 11, the LRP—that is, the probability that the entire portfolio will be exhausted before the random time of death—is 37.40%. This probability is obviously high, and the spending rate of 6% is clearly unsustainable. Note that even if the asset allocation is increased to 100% stocks, which has a higher expected return, the lifetime ruin probability is even higher. It results in an LRP of 37.82%. Similarly, if the risk exposure is reduced to 60% stocks, the value of the LRP is 39%, which is even worse. In summary, a $6-per-$100 spending rate from a portfolio at the age of 65 is unsustainable, unless the retiree expects much higher returns from the stock market than I have modeled here—an expected (arithmetic) return that exceeds 6% real return. Such a case would be hard to make in today's economic environment.

If the withdrawal rate is reduced to 3.5% while the asset allocation remains 80% stocks and 20% cash, Table 11 shows that the LRP drops to 9.98%, which is a failure rate of approximately 1 in 10. This probability might not be acceptable to everyone, but it is certainly more sustainable than a 6% spending rate.

Recall that all of these numbers and spending rates are in real (inflation-adjusted) terms, which reduces sustainability in comparison with nominal spending. If I were to assume a retiree spends a nominal (as opposed to real)

$60,000 per year from a $1,000,000 portfolio, then I would have to modify the (μ, σ, R) parameters and convert them into nominal terms. The LRP values would fall.

A number of other qualitative insights are worth noting from Table 11. First, the LRP is reduced with lower spending rates ($1/w$) and higher values of w. The relationship is monotonic. The same is not the case with asset allocation. Notice how at low spending rates, the LRP declines with increasing exposure to safe assets. At higher levels of spending, the LRP is U-shaped as a function of asset allocation. It is higher for much riskier and much safer allocations and is minimized in between 100% stocks and 100% safe cash. The intuition here is that further increasing exposure to stocks does not necessarily improve the odds of success because of the higher shortfall risk embedded in the portfolio.

In conclusion, the LRP is a summary risk metric that can help measure the sustainability of a retirement plan. The lower the LRP, the better. I want to be careful not to advocate LRP minimization, however, as a dynamic portfolio strategy. Rather, it should be viewed as yet another way of quantifying the benefit of annuitization. If you purchase a life annuity, the insurance company is on the hook regardless of how long you live or how the stock market performs. So—in this section's language—if the insurance company's credit is good, the LRP of the payout from a life annuity is zero.

Q22. How Does a Variable Immediate Annuity Work?

After reading the previous section on the odds that a diversified portfolio of stocks and bonds can beat a life annuity, you might naturally inquire whether you can actually reap the benefits of both the equity risk premium *and* mortality credits. Can you wrap a life annuity concept around a mix of stocks and bonds? The answer is a resounding yes, and it is the topic of this section.

Variable immediate annuities (VIAs), also known as "immediate variable annuities" or "variable payout annuities," are the "risky" counterpart to the "safe" life annuity. These products allow annuitants to (1) receive a lifetime of income they cannot outlive but also (2) have the ability to earn variable market-linked returns in the annuity structure. Technically, this feat is engineered by an insurance company paying out annuity *units*, as opposed to dollars and cents. Each year—or month, depending on the frequency of payment—the actual annuity payment is adjusted up or down in accord with how its underlying portfolio of stocks and bonds has performed. The number of units is fixed. Their value fluctuates. Moreover, the annuitant selects a balanced mixture of stock and bond funds (or subaccounts, in the parlance of insurance) and also picks a hurdle rate that must be achieved before payments will increase. If markets do better than the hurdle, cash flow increases. If it falls short, income shrinks.

The mechanics of a VIA seem tricky and obscure at first, so Equations 11a and 11b are provided to clear the fog. They display exactly how the annuity payments are adjusted on the basis of the investment portfolio's performance. Equation 11a addresses the baseline initial payout, c_0, as a function of the hurdle rate, and Equation 11b addresses how the payment is adjusted over time:

$$c_0 = \frac{W}{a(x,R)};$$ (11a)

$$c_i = \frac{c_{i-1}(1+R_i)}{1+R}.$$ (11b)

The symbol W denotes the initial premium (or wealth) used to purchase the variable immediate annuity. The familiar symbol $a(x, R)$ denotes the standard annuity factor under an "assumed" rate of interest (that is, the required hurdle rate). Finally, the actual return earned by the underlying investment portfolio is denoted by R_i and will determine the actual annuity payment. Notice that when $R_i > R$, the next period's payment, c_i, will increase, when $R_i < R$, the next payment will decline, and when $R_i = R$, the payment will remain unchanged.

Table 12 provides some numerical values for the baseline, Year 1, and Year 2 outcomes under various assumed investment returns (AIRs). For example, suppose you are a 65-year-old (male or female) who has purchased a VIA and has voluntarily selected an AIR of $R = 4\%$. According to the GAPM and Equation 11a, with parameters $m = 87.25$ and $b = 9.5$, the baseline annuity payment is \$7,820 per year. So, in theory, if the underlying investments in the VIA earned a fixed constant $R_i = 4\%$ every year (forever), your life annuity payment would remain at \$7,820 per year. Now, assume that during the first year—that is, between ages 65 and 66—the underlying portfolio of supporting investments earns $R_1 = 0\%$, which is 4 percentage points less than the hurdle rate, or AIR, of $R = 4\%$. In that case, the annuity payment drops by 4% and the annuity payment falls during the second year to \$7,519. Following through to the second year, if the investment return from the underlying portfolio is a loss of $R_2 = -25\%$, then the Year 2 payment drops by another 29% to \$5,423.

Note that for every year in which the investments earn less than the AIR hurdle, the annuity payment will drop. So, if you want to avoid a decline in income, you need to select the lowest AIR possible. Of course, doing so will increase the annuity factor, $a(x, R)$, which then will reduce the amount of the

Table 12. Payout from a VIA for Year 1 and Year 2

Year 1 Return (%)	Year 2 Return (%)	With AIR = 2%; Baseline Year 1 Payout = $6,420.00	With AIR = 4%; Baseline Year 1 Payout = $7,820.00	With AIR = 6%; Baseline Year 1 Payout = $9,340.00
$R_1 = -25$	NA	$4,720.59	$5,639.42	$6,608.49
$R_1 = 0$	NA	6,294.12	7,519.23	8,811.32
$R_1 = +25$	NA	7,867.65	9,399.04	11,014.15
$R_1 = -25$	$R_2 = -25$	3,471.02	4,066.89	4,675.82
$R_1 = -25$	$R_2 = 0$	4,628.03	5,422.52	6,234.43
$R_1 = -25$	$R_2 = +25$	5,785.03	6,778.15	7,793.03
$R_1 = 0$	$R_2 = -25$	4,628.03	5,422.52	6,234.43
$R_1 = 0$	$R_2 = 0$	6,170.70	7,230.03	8,312.57
$R_1 = 0$	$R_2 = +25$	7,713.38	9,037.54	10,390.71
$R_1 = +25$	$R_2 = -25$	5,785.03	6,778.15	7,793.03
$R_1 = +25$	$R_2 = 0$	7,713.38	9,037.54	10,390.71
$R_1 = +25$	$R_2 = +25$	9,641.72	11,296.92	12,988.39

Notes: The data are for a 65-year-old unisex. The GAPM parameters are $m = 87.25$ and $b = 9.5$. NA = not applicable.

initial baseline payment. So, if you choose a low AIR, your annuity income is less likely to be sabotaged by a down market, but it will be starting from a relatively low level of income.

If you select an AIR of 6% and during the first two years of retirement the underlying investment portfolio earns 25% in the first year and 25% in the second year, then Table 12 indicates that your annuity payment will grow to $12,988 by the time you are 67. In contrast, if you select, or opt for, a 2% AIR and the market drops by 25% in the first year and 25% in the second year, your annuity check will be $3,471 by age 67. Note the range of outcomes.

Another helpful way to think about a VIA is to view it as a *fixed* life annuity, but one that is paid in a foreign currency (euros or yen, for example). The payments are converted back into dollars at the prevailing exchange rate and paid out to the annuitant. So, if the currency has depreciated since the last payment was received, income will decline from a dollar perspective. But if the currency has strengthened since the last payment, the dollar value will increase. From a dollar perspective, the annuity income may appear to be fluctuating, but from the perspective of the foreign currency holder (and payer), the cash flows are fixed.

The same logic can be easily transferred to the VIA. The payments fluctuate in relation to the value of the underlying investment units, but from the perspective of the insurance company, the annuitant is entitled to a fixed number of units. In fact, insurance companies manufacture (and hedge) their obligations under a VIA in this manner.

Certainly, because of the market's behavior and the AIR selected, annuitants can expect a wide range of payments from a VIA. This wide range is probably one of the reasons that VIAs are not popular in practice among retirees. They are a tiny fraction of the market. Many people believe that retirement is a time for stable and predictable income. They do not want to be exposed to the ups and downs of the stock market. Therefore, some observers have said that a product with the words "variable income" and "annuity" in it is an oxymoron.

Of course, the annuitant can control the volatility of his or her income stream by selecting a more or less conservative allocation for the underlying investments supporting the annuity. In theory, he or she can allocate 100% of the money to safe money market funds, but if that is the annuitant's preference, a fixed immediate annuity—that is, a generic life annuity—might be more suitable.

In summary, the benefits of both longevity-risk pooling (that is, of mortality credits) and the equity risk premium may be obtained by purchasing a VIA instead of a fixed immediate annuity. Surprisingly, however, VIAs are even less popular than fixed annuities, possibly for behavioral reasons and possibly because of product complexity. Either way, one thing is certain: A life annuity *is not* an alternative to—nor does it compete with—a diversified portfolio of stocks and bonds. Rather, annuity payout characteristics can be overlaid on stock and bond returns (a VIA) or obtained independently of them (a fixed immediate annuity).

Q23. What Is the Difference between a Tontine and a Life Annuity?

According to the Merriam-Webster dictionary, a tontine is "a joint financial arrangement whereby the participants usually contribute equally to a prize that is awarded entirely to the participant who survives all the others." So, tontines and life annuities might appear to be similar, especially to those unfamiliar with longevity-contingent claims. Indeed, they both contain longevity insurance and protection against living "too long." Technically, both a tontine and a life annuity are a form of debt from the point of view of the issuer because a large sum of money is advanced to a financial institution, such as an insurance company (or even the king or queen in medieval times), entitling the investor to annual payments over the life of a nominee. The subtle difference between the two is exactly how those annual payments are determined and what happens when the nominee dies.

First, some notation is needed. Recall that for a fixed life annuity, the $a(x, R)$ denotes the annuity factor at age x under a valuation rate of R. (I have eliminated guarantee period g to keep things simple.) Recall that the annuity factor is the lump sum of money an x-year-old *investor* must pay in exchange for $1 of income during the rest of the *nominee's* life. In most cases, of course, the investor is the nominee:

$$a(x,R) = \sum_{t=1}^{\omega-x} \frac{p(x,t)}{(1+R)^t}. \tag{12a}$$

A critical point here is that upon death, the obligor (e.g., insurance company, government, or even the king and queen) is exempt from further payments. Many variations of Equation 12a are discussed in the literature, but the basic idea is the same: (1) The death of the nominee ends the life annuity, and (2) the investor does not care (aside from credit risk) how many other people have purchased similar life annuities. Every life is an entity unto itself.

With a tontine, however, an investor's peers and fellow annuitants play an important role. In a generic tontine, the investor is guaranteed to receive, for example, $1 of income for as long as the nominee is alive but the actual income received depends on the number of *other tontine nominees who die* during the year. Each death increases the surviving investors' income. So, for example, if 100 investor/nominees purchase tontine units paying $1 per year for life, the nominee pool consists of $100 per year. Then, 10 years later, if only 50 nominees are alive in the tontine pool, the surviving investors get to share the $100, which is a payment of $2 per investor. Then, 20 years later, if only 10 nominees remain in the tontine pool, the surviving investors get $10 of income each. With a tontine, you and the other nominees are guaranteed the $1 of income but the upside potential is enormous as long as you are still alive. (No wonder tontine schemes have spurred the imagination of crime writers for centuries.)

To investigate the math for the tontine, let $o(x, R)$ denote the tontine factor at age x with a valuation rate of R. Each tontine unit—paying at least $1 for life—will cost $o(x, R)$ dollars up front. So, in parallel with the definition of annuity factor, the tontine factor is

$$o(x,R) = \sum_{t=1}^{\omega-x} \frac{1}{(1+R)^t}$$
$$= \frac{1-(1+R)^{-(\omega-x)}}{R}. \tag{12b}$$

Note the difference between Equations 12a and 12b: $o(x, R) > a(x, R)$ because there is no survival probability, $p(x, t) < 1$, in the numerator of the tontine factor. In fact, $o(x, R)$ is simply the present value factor of a term certain annuity paid over $(\omega - x)$ years. Intuitively, there is no mortality in the formula because the obligor must continue to make payments to the pool regardless of who is alive. As long as even one nominee is still alive, the payment to the tontine pool continues. The tontine is effectively a term certain fixed annuity to the obligor, but with a miniscule amount of risk that depends on the longest lived annuitant—the term of the annuity.[26]

To monitor the size of the tontine pool, let $N(x, t)$ denote the number of original tontine nominees at age x who are still alive in year t. Naturally, $N(x, t)$ will decline over time, and eventually, once the entire group has died off, $N(x, \omega - x)$ will equal zero. The actual tontine payment to the survivors will be a multiple of the ratio between the original nominees and the number of survivors: $N(x, 0)/N(x, t)$.

Here is an example of the mechanics. Let's assume a group of x number of 50-year-olds and a valuation rate of $R = 6\%$ per year. As for the mortality probability, $p(x, t)$, let's assume that the individual survival probability obeys a Gompertz distribution with the modal value $m = 86.549$ and dispersion value $b = 10$. This parameterization implies that $p(50, 45) = 10\%$, and everyone is dead by age $\omega = 120$.

Let's assume now that you (as both investor and nominee) are 50 years old and have a choice between purchasing a life annuity paying $1 a year for life and a tontine paying (at least) $1 a year for life. According to Equation 12a, the life annuity will cost $13.303. So, an investment of $1,000 will result in a constant payment of $75.17 (1,000/13.303) for life. This payment is a yield of 7.517%, which is 1.5 percentage points above the 6% valuation rate because of the mortality credits. So far, nothing is new.

The tontine, according to Equation 12b, will cost $16.3845 per unit and will entitle the nominee to (at least) $1 of income per year for life, with the potential for more depending on the survival of other nominees. An investment of $1,000 will lead to 1,000/16.3845 = $61.03 (at least) per year for life. **Table 13** displays results under the assumption that 1,000 people each contribute $1,000 dollars for a total of $1,000,000. The $61,030 per year benefit to the pool of nominees—assumed to be made for a total of 70 years—is split among all survivors. The last survivor then keeps the entire $61,030 each year until he or she dies. For example, although there is only a 61% chance that a 50-year-old nominee/investor will survive to age 80, if he or she does actually live for 30 years but only $N(50, 30) = 610$ other members of the tontine pool survive, the nominee/investor will be entitled to a payout of $99.98. This is $25 more than what the life annuity would provide. And if a mere $N(50, 30) = 488$ members of the original pool of 1,000 nominees survive, the tontine income becomes $124.98.

---

[26]More information is available in my forthcoming manuscript tentatively entitled "Tontines: How a Fascinating but Neglected Annuity Scheme Can Help Reduce the Cost of Retirement."

Table 13. Tontine vs. Life Annuity Payouts over Time: $1,000 Invested at Age 50

Age	Estimated Survival Probability	Actual No. of Survivors	Annual Tontine Payout	Annual Annuity Payout
Year 5 (i.e., age 55)	98.34%	1,000	$61.03	$75.17
		983	62.07	75.17
		787	77.58	75.17
Year 10 (i.e., age 60)	95.65	1,000	61.03	75.17
		956	63.81	75.17
		765	79.76	75.17
Year 30 (i.e., age 80)	61.04	732	83.32	75.17
		610	99.98	75.17
		488	124.98	75.17
Year 45 (i.e., age 95)	10.00	120	508.42	75.17
		100	610.10	75.17
		80	762.63	75.17

In the tontine, you gain from others' misfortune, which creates some interesting moral (and mortal) hazard problems.

To conclude, although tontines were extremely popular in medieval Europe—and actually proposed by Alexander Hamilton, the first U.S. secretary of the Treasury, as a way to reduce U.S. debt—they are currently illegal in most developed countries. This book is not the place to delve into the reasons for the tontine bans and whether they are justified in today's environment, but you can certainly see the appeal of tontines over annuities for someone like Methuselah. Perhaps they will be in vogue again someday.

3. The Scholarly Literature

The scholarly (academic and practitioner) literature on the topic of life annuities is vast and growing. As of late 2012, I counted somewhere in the vicinity of 2,000 research articles (based on Google scholar citations) written during the past 50 years that could be considered part of an extended field of annuity literature. Thus, listing, mentioning, or giving credit to all of them is impossible. I have done my best to narrow down the list of relevant research to approximately 200 key articles. The filters I used for inclusion were *articles on life annuities that would be relevant to private wealth managers, institutional asset managers, and pension plan sponsors as well as scholars conducting research in this area.*

To refine and organize this task, I separated the list of 200 or so research articles into six streams or subfields in the life annuity literature. Although some overlaps exist between the groups, I believe the articles can be classified along the following general lines:

1. *The life-cycle model of saving and consumption*, which acknowledges that the length of life is random rather than fixed and studies conditions in a world in which life annuities are not necessarily available. This stream of literature is concerned with the impact of (pure) longevity risk on rational consumer behavior and with the way consumers behave once life annuities are introduced into the opportunity set. The first formal discussions in the economics literature are Fisher (1930) and Yaari (1965). I also include in this section articles that tie annuities to the capital asset pricing model (Sharpe 1964 and other authors).

2. *The pricing, valuation, hedging, and reserving of life annuities.* If you seek a first paper in this subfield, it is the key article by Halley (1693). Articles in this genre are actuarial and technical in nature. They will be discussed and referenced only insofar as they relate to the (theoretical) cost of annuities for individuals.

3. *The optimal allocation and timing of annuitization.* This subfield is closest to the traditional investment asset allocation literature in that it attempts to derive, in a normative fashion, the optimal amount of personal wealth that should be allocated to a life annuity and the best time (and age) to annuitize. This research is usually embedded in a rational, utility-maximizing life-cycle framework similar to the multiperiod asset allocation literature pioneered by Samuelson (1969) and Merton (1971). The Yaari (1965) article is key to this stream as well the first group mentioned, but the focus is on modern "portfolio choice" models as opposed to the theoretical optimality of life annuities.

4. *The formulation and solution of the annuity puzzle.* This group, by far the largest subfield in the annuity literature, addresses the (puzzling) phenomenon that few people actually choose to annuitize. The puzzle was first identified formally by Modigliani (1986), but can actually be traced to Huebner (1927). Although this genre is labeled a "puzzle," most of the recent articles I will reference argue that it might (now) be less puzzling than previously thought.

5. *The money's worth ratio of actual annuity prices in the United States and around the world.* This subfield, first introduced by Friedman and Warshawsky (1990), is an attempt to compare actual prices with model prices and to measure goodness of fit, efficiency, and other metrics of concern to economists. The money's worth ratio was explained in Chapter 2; the literature review will provide an opportunity to showcase the large numbers of researchers who use this metric.

6. *Articles that do not fit neatly into the preceding categories.* No key or first article comes to mind for this category. It is a bit of a catchall for research articles that do not belong in the other categories and is presented last for that reason.

In each category discussion, the key research articles are given chronologically. Generally, relevant excerpts provide key insights from the articles in the authors' own words.

The Life-Cycle Model and Life Annuities

Most experts agree that the economics of annuities research begins with the life-cycle work of Fisher (1930)—in particular, his following comments:

> The shortness of life thus tends powerfully to increase the degree of impatience, or rate of time preference, beyond what it would otherwise be. This is especially evident when the income streams compared are long . . . But whereas the shortness and uncertainty of life tend to increase impatience, their effect is greatly mitigated by . . . solicitude for the welfare of one's heirs. Probably the most powerful cause tending to reduce the rate of interest is the love of one's children and the desire to provide for their good. (p. 52)

The next step in the evolution of this literature was the classical paper duo by Yaari (1964, 1965). While still a doctoral candidate at Stanford University, under the supervision of Nobel laureate Kenneth Arrow. Yaari was the first economist to introduce annuities into the life-cycle model, which is commonly linked to Modigliani or Friedman. Yaari's 1965 research paper is the most widely cited research article in the life annuity economics literature.

In the 1960s, academic economists had not really given any thought to how length-of-lifetime uncertainty—and the randomness of the length of retirement, in particular—affects financial planning, saving, and investment behavior. Fisher and some others had some vague notions that old age might make people (cranky and) impatient, but they had nothing concrete or formal.

Around the same time, modern portfolio theory, introduced by Markowitz, was starting to catch on with academics. (It would be decades before the idea reached Wall Street.) But even Markowitz, and his contemporary Sharpe, did not until recently address how the randomness of life might affect economic behavior and portfolio construction. Two other economic giants of the time, Friedman (1957) and Modigliani (1986), theorized that consumers like to smooth their standard of living over time in consideration of their lifetime resources. Neither of them said anything about mortality and longevity. In most of their models and papers, people died at a fixed and known time.

Yaari, writing his PhD at Stanford University in the early 1960s, started his famous 1965 paper with the following words:

> One need hardly be reminded that a consumer who makes plans for the future must, in one way or another, take account of the fact that he does not know how long he will live. Yet, few discussions of consumer allocation over time give this problem due consideration. Alfred Marshall and Irving Fisher were both aware of the uncertainty of survival, but for one reason or another they did not expound on how a consumer might be expected to react to this uncertainty if he is to behave *rationally*. (p. 137)

Yaari went on to describe how consumers would slowly spend down their wealth in proportion to their survival probabilities and attitudes to longevity risk and gradually reduce their standard of living—rationally. But then, if you gave these same consumers the ability to purchase any type of annuity desired, they would not have to reduce their standard of living with age. They would, in fact, be able to hedge or insure against their longevity risk. He then went one step further and derived the optimal "portfolio mix" between regular market-based instruments (e.g., mutual funds) and their actuarial counterparts (life annuities) as a function of an individual's preference for bequest versus consumption in his or her own lifetime. In modern terms, he introduced what I call "product allocation" only a few years after Markowitz introduced "asset allocation." The Yaari paper has been cited thousands of times by economic scholars in the 45 years since it was published.[27] Yaari, Sharpe, and Markowitz are all still alive.[28]

---

[27]Quite justifiably, some people refer to Yaari as "the Harry Markowitz" of the annuity world.
[28]Most recently, Yaari was president of the Israeli Academy of Sciences and Humanities.

Figure 4 illustrates how one would rationally spend down wealth in a life-cycle model, especially during the retirement years. Each of the four curves represents a different level of longevity-risk aversion. The *y*-axis represents the annual consumption rate, and the *x*-axis represents the age of the retiree. For example, according to the graph, an individual with a very low longevity-risk aversion (i.e., longevity-risk tolerant) would spend at a rate of $14 per $100 dollars in his first year of retirement. Then, as time passes, he would reduce his consumption rate until the nest egg was depleted at age 90 and would live off his pension of $5 per year. In contrast, someone with very high longevity-risk aversion, which is the lowest of the four curves displayed, would start off spending much less in retirement—$10 per year—and she would reduce her spending over time only very slowly, so she would still have liquid wealth and assets at the age of 100. Figure 4 thus shows the essence of longevity-risk aversion: The fear that you might live a very long time leads to you spending less as a result. I refer

Figure 4. Life-Cycle Consumption during Retirement as a Function of Longevity-Risk Aversion

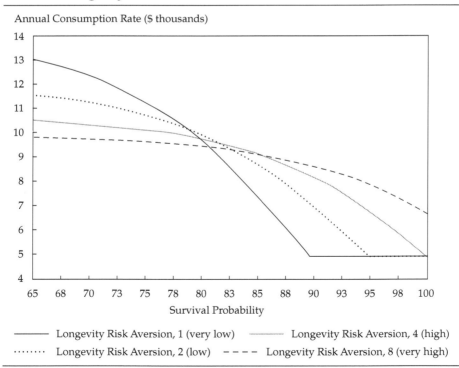

Source: Based on data from Milevsky and Huang (2011), p. 51.

©2013 The Research Foundation of CFA Institute

the interested reader to Milevsky and Huang (2011) for more information on how longevity-risk aversion affects spending rates in the presence of pension and life annuity income.

To sum up, Yaari (1965) would have the individual reducing consumption in proportion to his or her survival probability and then eventually depleting wealth and living off pension and annuity income alone. The greater the amount of pension and annuity income, the earlier the person's wealth would be depleted. Similarly, the greater the person's longevity-risk tolerance, the earlier wealth would be depleted.

One of the most frequently quoted results attributed to Yaari (1965) is that life annuities are not only an important component of a consumer's portfolio but should also actually form the entirety of the portfolio in the absence of a bequest or legacy motive. He pointed out that the mortality credits are simply too valuable to ignore. Yet, as noted earlier, few people actively choose to annuitize any portion of their nest egg, much less all of it.

In a seminar that Yaari gave at the IFID Centre at the Fields Institute in 2010 to commemorate his work in the area, he mentioned that his 1965 paper was originally intended to help resolve inconsistencies in neoclassical economics and the apparent low spend-down rate of assets around retirement. In that sense, his paper was intended as "positive" (to explain observed behavior) as opposed to "normative" (to provide financial advice). In other words, he never intended to write a manifesto on how people should behave in the face of lifetime uncertainty—namely, that they should hedge longevity risk by purchasing annuities. At the same time, he acknowledged that this model can easily be inverted and used to offer guidance on how people should allocate their assets around retirement.

The next influential paper in this literature was written by Hakansson (1969). Echoing the work by Yaari (1964, 1965), Hakansson argued, "Any given individual may be able to make himself better off both by the purchase of insurance on his own life and the sale of insurance on the lives of others" (p. 444).

A further advance in the literature on life-cycle planning and lifetime uncertainty was a 1973 paper by Fischer. He stated:

> An individual who receives labor income is more likely to purchase insurance than an individual who lives off the proceeds of his wealth. If insurance is fair, then—in the consumption decision—future income is discounted at the safe rate and weighted by the probability of being alive to receive it in reducing it to comparability with wealth . . . An individual who lives off the proceeds of his wealth is unlikely ever to purchase life insurance. An individual who receives labor income is likely to purchase life insurance early in his life. In all simulations the individual tends to sell life insurance late in life: Institutional reasons why companies do not engage in such transactions exist. The purchase of

annuities generates consumption and bequest patterns similar to those of the simulations. Multiperiod term insurance either presents the individual with arbitrage possibilities, or makes no difference to his welfare. (p. 148)

Another important paper in this vein is that of Richard (1975), who embedded the Merton (1971) model into the Yaari (1964) model and stated:

> A continuous time model for optimal consumption, portfolio and life insurance rules, for an investor with an arbitrary but known distribution of lifetime, is derived as a generalization of the model by Merton (1971). The investor is found to have a "human capital" component of wealth, which is independent of his preferences and risky market opportunities and represents the certainty equivalent of his future net (wage) earnings. (p. 187)

In other words, the existence of annuities and insurance allows for the valuation of the human capital stream.

Barro and Friedman (1977) contrasted consumer choice under uncertain lifetimes with the behavior that would arise if each individual's lifetime were announced at birth. In a model that included life insurance and excluded investments in human capital, they found that

> the expected utility under uncertain lifetimes exceeds that under known lifetimes when the latter expectation is based on preannouncement survival probabilities. This conclusion emerges, first, because the model without human capital contains no planning benefits from knowledge of the horizon and, second, because the prior announcement of lifetimes forces risk-averse consumers to undertake an extra gamble that they could otherwise avoid by using life insurance. (p. 843)

Once again, the role of life annuities emerges in a life-cycle model by creating certainty out of horizon uncertainty.

Mirer (1979) was one of the first to document that retirees were not spending down wealth at the rate you might expect from a life-cycle model. They simply weren't spending enough, possibly (given the random length of life) because they were worried about outliving their wealth.

Davies (1981) investigated whether

> the continued accumulation, or mild dissaving, observed among the retired can be explained by uncertain lifetime. In the absence of annuities, after an initial period influenced by borrowing constraints, under constant relative risk aversion, uncertain lifetime depresses consumption by a proportion increasing with age if the elasticity of inter-temporal substitution in consumption is "small." Illustrative computations, based on actual income and survival data, show that plausible elasticities are sufficiently small to give this effect. The reduction in consumption is large enough to explain much of the lack of decumulation by the elderly. (p. 561)

In other words, Davies believes that people who do not have access to life annuities—or refuse to use them—need more money to finance their retirement than they would if they had access to life annuities.

Kotlikoff and Spivak (1981) took a slightly different approach to the topic by examining risk sharing in families as an alternative to annuities. They wrote:

> Consumption and bequest-sharing arrangements within marriage and larger families can substitute to a large extent for complete and fair annuity markets. In the absence of such public markets, individuals have strong economic incentives to establish relationships which provide risk-mitigating opportunities. Within marriages and families there is a degree of trust, information, and love which aids in the enforcement of risk-sharing agreements. Our calculations indicate that pooling the risk of death can be an important economic incentive for family formation; the paper also suggests that the current instability in family arrangements may, to some extent, reflect recent growth in pension and social security public annuities. (p. 388)

In other words, if you have a large enough family to help share the burden and the risk, you might not need life annuities.[29] This line of thinking was pursued also in Kotlikoff, Shoven, and Spivak (1986).

Bernheim (1984) argued that

> actuarial valuation of annuity benefit streams is theoretically inconsistent with the assumption of pure life-cycle motives. Instead, we show that the simple discounted value of future benefits (ignoring the possibility of death) is often a good approximation to the relevant concept of value. This observation motivates a re-examination of existing empirical evidence concerning the effects of Social Security on personal savings, retirement, and the distribution of wealth, as well as the proper computation of age–wealth profiles. (p. 1)

In a series of papers, Eckstein, Eichenbaum, and Peled (1985a, 1985b) examined

> the implications of the absence of complete annuity markets on the distribution of wealth and the welfare of agents who make savings decisions under uncertainty regarding the length of their life . . . The absence of annuity markets has, in addition to its other effects, potentially important implications for the equilibrium distribution of wealth. In particular, the existence of annuity markets ensures a degenerate distribution of wealth across individuals.[30] On the other hand, the absence of such markets results in the inequality of wealth across members of the same generation . . . This inequality is not a transient phenomenon; the unique steady state distribution of wealth is nondegenerate. (1985b, p. 789)

---

[29]And perhaps if you have enough annuity income, you might not bother acquiring a family.
[30]In this context, "degenerate" means nonsmooth distribution.

In a related paper, Eckstein, Eichenbaum, and Peled (1985a) explored the implications of social security programs and annuity markets through which agents, who are characterized by different distributions of length of lifetime, share death-related risks. They found:

> When annuity markets operate, a nondiscriminatory social security program affects only the intragenerational allocation of resources. In the absence of private information regarding individual survival probabilities, such a program will lead to a nonoptimal intragenerational allocation of resources. However, the presence of adverse selection considerations gives rise to a Pareto improving role for a mandatory nondiscriminatory social security program.[31] (p. 303)

If a life-cycle model that assumes rational and optimizing behavior is to have practical application, an extremely important question is, Are individuals capable of formulating coherent expectations about their longevity and mortality probabilities? Hamermesh (1985) addresses this point. He examined the awareness of demographic changes by individuals as they projected their life expectancies and survival probabilities. He studied whether their projections were based on determinants that coincided with the evidence of epidemiological and demographic studies. Hamermesh concluded:

> Most important, I find that people do extrapolate changing life tables when they determine their subjective horizons, and they are aware of levels of and improvements within current life tables . . . They base their subjective life expectancies disproportionately on their relatives' longevity. (p. 404)

Along the same lines, Hurd (1989) found:

> The consumption path is sensitive to variations in mortality rates, meaning that mortality risk aversion is moderate and certainly much smaller than what is typically assumed in the literature. The marginal utility of bequests is small; therefore, desired bequests, which are estimated from model simulations, are small on average. Apparently most bequests are accidental, the result of uncertainty about the date of death. The parameter estimates imply that although consumption and wealth paths may rise at early ages, eventually they will fall as mortality rates become large. (p. 779)

In an interesting paper that seems to contradict the spirit of the Yaari (1965) result, Pecchenino and Pollard (1997) examined the effects of introducing actuarially fair annuity markets into a model of endogenous growth with overlapping generations. They found:

> The complete annuitisation of agents' wealth is not, in general, dynamically optimal; the degree of annuitisation that is dynamically optimal depends nonmonotonically on the expected length of retirement and on the pay-as-you-go

---

[31]"Adverse selection" refers to the fact that annuitants live longer than the rest of the population. A "nondiscriminatory social security program" is one in which redistribution is minimized.

©2013 The Research Foundation of CFA Institute

social security tax rate. The government has an incentive to restrict the availability of actuarially fair annuity contracts, and can often move the economy from a pay-as-you-go to a fully funded social security system via voluntary contributions to a government sponsored, actuarially fair pension today accompanied by reductions in social security taxes tomorrow. (p. 26)

Clearly, introducing multiple (overlapping) generations into the life-cycle model can actually overturn some of the established results regarding the optimality of annuities in a model based on a single representative agent.

As I have argued in numerous places in this book, life annuities are a form of pension. And a number of researchers in the life-cycle literature have built on that idea. Sundaresan and Zapatero (1997) provide a framework linking the valuation and asset allocation policies of defined benefit plans with the lifetime marginal productivity schedule of the worker and the pension plan formula. They stated:

Our model provides an explicit valuation formula for a stylized defined benefits plan. The optimal asset allocation policies consist of the replicating portfolio of the pension liabilities and the growth optimum portfolio independent of the pension liabilities. We show that the worker will retire when the ratio of pension benefits to current wages reaches a critical value which depends on the parameters of the pension plan and the discount rate.[32] (p. 631)

As I have stressed, individuals who are unwilling to trade the bequest motive and liquidity in exchange for mortality credits will not value the life annuity. This assertion can be shown rigorously in a life-cycle model. For example, Jousten (2001) stated that "consumption is non-increasing in the linear bequest parameter for the simplest certainty case" (p. 149). He found the same was not true for lifespan uncertainty. Jousten also studied the issue of annuity valuation and found that "for a sufficiently strong bequest motive, the true value of an annuity is equal to the actuarial value" (p. 149). In other words, a standard fixed-income bond would be preferable for those individuals with strong enough bequest motives.

It is not only the bequest motive that can affect annuitization in a life-cycle framework. Babbel and Merrill (2007b) modeled individual behavior "under the possibility of default by the insurer issuing annuities" (p. 1). They found that even a little default risk can have a huge impact on annuity purchase decisions. Furthermore, state insolvency guarantee programs can have a big impact on the level of rational life annuity purchases.

---

[32]Sundaresan and Zapatero (1997) thus set forth a kind of liability-based capital asset pricing model (CAPM), a path taken by Waring (2004a, 2004b). In this literature, a life annuity (or, more generally, a fixed-income instrument with cash flows matched to the investor's liability) is considered the risk-free asset, whereas in the original CAPM, cash is the risk-free asset.

Yet another deterrent to annuitization in a life-cycle model would be government pensions that, implicitly, already provide annuities. This situation might also affect retirement behavior. For example, Jiménez-Martín and Sánchez Martín (2007) explored the effects of the minimum pension program in Spain on welfare and retirement. They used data from the Spanish social security system to estimate the behavioral parameters of the model and then simulated the changes induced by the minimum pension in aggregate retirement patterns. They found that the impact is substantial: "There is a threefold increase in retirement at 60, the age of first entitlement, with respect to the economy without minimum pensions, and total early retirement (before or at 60) is almost 50% larger" (p. 923).

Continuing on the relationship between social security pensions and life annuities, Sheshinski (2007) demonstrated rigorously that "a public social security system may be socially superior to private annuity markets" (p. 251). Of course, the public social security system would have to be "large" enough to fully cover even the wealthiest of individuals.

Now, because U.S. Social Security and the Canadian Pension Plan are mandatory program, you might wonder how its compulsory nature affects the welfare of retirees. Motivated by this issue, Gong and Webb (2008) investigated the distributional consequences of mandatory annuitization. Using the University of Michigan Health and Retirement Study data and accounting for longevity-risk pooling within marriage and preannuitized wealth, they found substantial redistribution away from disadvantaged groups in expected-utility terms. They used a life-cycle model to calculate the value each household would place on annuitization, based on the husband's and wife's subjective life tables, and the household's degree of risk aversion and proportion of preannuitized wealth. Their conclusion is that "a significant minority would perceive themselves as suffering a loss from mandatory annuitization" (p. 1055).

A growing recent literature attempts to calibrate the life-cycle model to actual data—for groups both with and without access to annuities—to examine whether mandatory markets affect consumption. Hansen and İmrohoroğlu (2008) stated:

> In our calibrated model, if complete annuity markets exist, consumption would increase over the entire life-cycle. When the annuity market is shut down, consumption displays a hump shape where consumption peaks well before retirement. Social security, because it substitutes for the missing annuity market, causes consumption to continue increasing until after retirement, although consumption still displays a hump shape. In particular, the consumption profile displayed by our model peaks significantly later than what has been estimated from U.S. consumption data. We find that these

conclusions are robust to the introduction of a bequest motive calibrated to account for the fraction of wealth held by the elderly, although consumption now peaks at a somewhat lower age. (p. 582)

Lachance (2012) analyzed a similar life-cycle model, one in which the optimal wealth depletion time was derived and calibrated.

A study along the same lines is Finkelstein, Poterba, and Rothschild (2009), in which the authors calibrated and solved a model of the U.K. compulsory annuity market and examined the impact of gender-based pricing restrictions. They wrote: "Our findings indicate the importance of endogenous contract responses and illustrate the feasibility of using theoretical insurance market equilibrium models for quantitative policy analysis" (p. 38). In other words, much can be learned from the responses of individuals to a wide choice of similar insurance policies covering differing risks.

Finally, McCarthy and Mitchell (2010), like Finkelstein et al. (2009), focused on the role of adverse selection (the fact that annuitants live longer than the rest of the population) and examined equilibrium pricing and demand implications. According to McCarthy and Mitchell, in the absence of insurance company underwriting, adverse selection improves the mortality of annuity purchasers but worsens that of purchasers of other life insurance products relative to the general population. (By "improve," they obviously do not mean that buying the annuity makes them healthier but, rather, that the pool of buyers tends to be healthier when there is no underwriting.) They explored the differences between mortality tables for this group in the United States, the United Kingdom, and Japan. They found:

> Adverse selection reduces mortality for both life insurance and annuities, contrary to what theory would suggest. This indicates that insurance company screening of potential poorer risks in classic life insurance ("underwriting") is effective, possibly even eliminating any asymmetric information held by policyholders. (p. 120)

The common thread among the papers surveyed and discussed thus far is their use of a life-cycle model of saving and consumption to investigate the implications of length-of-life uncertainty, both with and without annuity markets. I now consider the second strand in the annuity literature, which has to do with pricing.

Actuarial Pricing, Valuation, and Reserving

Possibly the first published paper to formally demonstrate how to price a life annuity is Halley (1693)—yes, the Edmond Halley of comet fame. His paper incorporated mortality into the time value of money. He wrote:

It is plain that the purchaser ought to pay for only such a part of the value of the annuity as he has chances that he is living; and this ought to be computed yearly, and the sum of all those yearly values being added together, will amount to the value of the annuity for the life of the person proposed. (p. 602)

More than 320 years of actuarial literature and models have flowed from this statement.

Most observers trace the invention of the variable immediate annuity (VIA) to Duncan (1952). His objective was to supplement fixed annuities, which are susceptible to inflation, with annuities that would increase over time. His proposal was to

provide pensions which will, insofar as possible, increase when prices are high. Of course, this carries with it the probability of decrease when prices are low. The purpose of this paper is to describe this novel type of corporation, which presents some unusual and interesting actuarial problems. A general explanation of the Fund will first be presented, followed by a summary of the statistical data compiled in developing it. Finally, there is given a detailed presentation of the actuarial plan to be used, involving the accumulation units and annuity units on which the Fund's annuities are to be based. (p. 318)

The Gompertz annuity pricing model (GAPM), which was described in Chapter 2, can be traced to Mereu (1962). He wrote that

the formula for evaluating annuities on a Makeham mortality table, should be satisfactory for making calculations recognizing calendar year of birth as a factor, provided the improvement in mortality is anticipated in such a manner that the generation mortality table for each year of birth follows Makeham's Law. (p. 286)

A financial view of life annuity pricing is offered by Broverman (1986), who examined aspects of the distribution of the internal rate for standard life insurance and annuity contracts. Another important actuarial paper in the pricing literature was written by Beekman and Fuelling (1990). They developed a model for certain annuities that can be used when interest rates and future lifetimes are random. A related actuarial paper is Frees, Carriere, and Valdez (1996), who investigated the impact of dependent mortality models—often called the "broken heart syndrome"—when valuing annuities. They found that annuity values are reduced by approximately 5 when dependent mortality models are used rather than the standard models that assume independence. In other words, if market prices fully adjusted for this effect, married couples would be able to obtain 5% more income than markets (and models) take into account. Frees et al. used a GAPM, and Carriere, in particular, was an early advocate of this model. In a related paper, Carriere (1999) wrote:

Using a no-arbitrage argument, the classical actuarial valuation formulas for life insurance and annuities are consistent with no-arbitrage pricing, assuming that the time of death is stochastically independent of the market prices on bonds. (p. 339)

Moving on to the valuation of guarantees in variable annuity (VA) policies, which offer the option to annuitize, Milevsky and Promislow (2001) argued, "The insurance company has essentially granted the policyholder an option on two underlying stochastic variables: future interest rates and future mortality rates" (p. 299). They developed a model in which both mortality and interest rate risk can be hedged and the option to annuitize can be priced by locating a replicating portfolio involving insurance, annuities, and default-free bonds. Similar techniques were used by Milevsky and Posner (2001) to value guaranteed minimum death benefit (GMDB) options in VAs. They wrote that

a simple return-of-premium death benefit is worth between one and ten basis points, depending on gender, purchase age, and asset volatility. In contrast, the median Mortality and Expense risk charge for return-of-premium variable annuities is 115 bps. In other words, consumers were overpaying for this guarantee. (p. 93)

Mudavanhu and Zhuo (2002) argue that the lapse option, which is the option to simply walk away from the VA and surrender its cash value, significantly increases the value of the GMDB option. Both the lapse and the death benefit options are much more valuable for middle-aged and older investors than for younger investors because of the insurance fees.

Most of the subsequent research concluded that the embedded guarantees are underpriced. Examples are Boyle and Hardy (2003) and Ballotta and Haberman (2003). The guaranteed lifetime withdrawal benefit (GLWB) and its close cousin, the guaranteed minimum withdrawal benefit (GMWB) with a fixed-maturity horizon, was formally analyzed by Milevsky and Salisbury (2006). The GMWB promises to return the entire initial investment, albeit spread over an extended period of time, regardless of subsequent market performance. The main result in Milevsky and Salisbury is that "the No Arbitrage hedging cost of a GMWB ranges from 73–160 bps of assets. In contrast, most products in the market only charge 30–45 bps" (p. 21). The authors concluded their article by arguing that pricing—in 2005 and 2006, when the article was written—was not sustainable and that GMWB fees would eventually have to increase or product design would have to change to avoid blatant arbitrage opportunities. This prediction did, in fact, come true as most large insurance companies scaled back or completely withdrew from this market. In some cases, no equilibrium fee will cover this risk.

Similar "underpricing" conclusions were reached by Chen, Vetzal, and Forsyth (2008). They wrote:

Only if several unrealistic modeling assumptions are made is it possible to obtain GMWB fees in the same range as is normally charged. In all other cases, it would appear that typical fees are not enough to cover the cost of hedging these guarantees. (p. 165)

Related research was conducted by Dai, Kwok, and Zong (2008). They used singular stochastic control methods for pricing variable annuities with the GMWB and also examined optimal withdrawal policies for holders of the VAs with the GMWB.

Shah and Bertsimas (2008) examined annuities with GLWBs and claimed, "GLWB has insufficient price discrimination and is susceptible to adverse selection . . . Valuations can vary substantially depending on which class of model is used" (p. 1). Shah and Bertsimas echoed the works of Milevsky and Salisbury (2006) and of Chen et al. (2008) by concluding that the product can be challenging to hedge and should create concerns for the insurance companies offering the guarantees.

Another strand in the valuation, pricing, and hedging literature addresses the concept of natural hedges and possible securitization of longevity risk in life annuities and similar insurance products. Lin and Cox (2005) wrote, "Securitization in the annuity and life insurance markets has been relatively rare, but we have argued that this may change" (p. 247). In related work about hedging longevity risk in life annuities, Cox and Lin (2007) argued, "The values of life insurance and annuity liabilities move in opposite directions in response to a change in the underlying mortality. Natural hedging utilizes this to stabilize aggregate liability cash flows" (p. 1). This statement is more than theoretical. The authors claimed to find empirical evidence suggesting that annuity writing insurers who have more balanced business in life and annuity risks also tend to charge lower premiums than otherwise similar insurers.

In a review paper on the analysis of longevity risk using stochastic modeling techniques from finance, Cairns, Blake, and Dowd (2008) offered a broad review and considered the wide range of extrapolative stochastic mortality models that have been proposed in the past 15–20 years. A number of models that they considered are framed in discrete time and emphasize the statistical aspects of modeling and forecasting. The 2008 paper by this trio is one of the most comprehensive articles on the topic. In follow-up work, Dowd, Blake, and Cairns (2011) proposed computationally efficient algorithms for quantifying the impact of interest rate risk and longevity risk on the distribution of annuity values in the distant future. They made the argument that annuity values are likely to rise considerably but are also uncertain. By "annuity value," they meant the actual cost of receiving $1 of income per year for life. Remember that the annuity value is the inverse of the annuity payout. If annuity values are likely to rise, according to the authors, then the monthly payouts (yields) are likely to decline.

Macdonald and McIvor (2010) fall into the category of predicting or forecasting future prices for life annuities but from a medical and biological perspective. They considered a number of gene variants that have been found to affect longevity. Using an annuity pricing model, they found that possibly significant uncertainty about annuity premiums may be overlooked if the standard errors of parameters estimated in medical studies are ignored by medical underwriters. They concluded with some policy implications:

> Such considerations may play an important part when the acceptability of using a risk factor in underwriting is conditional on proof of its relevance and reliability. This is the current position in respect of genetic information in many countries, most prominently in the United Kingdom. (p. 1)

Related research was conducted by Kwon and Jones (2006). They showed that "extended risk classification enables insurers to provide more equitable life insurance and annuity benefits for individuals in different risk classes and to manage mortality/longevity risk more efficiently" (p. 271). Like Macdonald and McIvor (2010), they argued that "mortality differentials resulted in a noticeable impact on actuarial values for different risk classes" (p. 287).

Finally, for those interested in a textbook-level introduction to actuarial pricing models in general and the valuation of more complicated life annuities in particular, the two leading texts in this area are Promislow (2011) and Dickson, Hardy, and Waters (2009). Both texts provide a comprehensive introduction to actuarial mathematics covering deterministic and stochastic models of life contingencies and covering advanced topics, such as risk theory, credibility theory, and multistate models.

Optimal Product Allocation and Timing

The questions of (1) when to annuitize and (2) how much to allocate to a life annuity were first addressed in the classic paper by Yaari (1965), who found that in the absence of bequest motives and other market imperfections, 100% of wealth should be annuitized, immediately. This paper was the first to offer a recommended allocation to an insurance product—that is, "product allocation" in contrast to investment "asset allocation." Numerous papers on optimal allocations followed during the next 50 years, and I will do my best to survey them in chronological order.

Buser and Smith (1983) wrote that

> insuring against the loss of a claim on future earnings as a result of the wage-earner's death may be modeled as a portfolio problem in which the return on a life insurance contract is negatively correlated with the return on the claim.

The model yields a result which expresses the optimal amount of life insurance in terms of two components: the value of the claim to be protected and the investment characteristics of the insurance contract. (p. 147)

Their result is obviously quite general and could be related to both life insurance and life annuities.

Sinha (1986) is another early paper to examine the impact of survival probabilities, loadings, interest rates, and bequest motives on the demand for life annuities in an optimal portfolio framework.

Brugiavini (1993) developed a model in which consumers have the option to purchase annuities before learning their survival probability. The model then allows consumers to recontract the initial choice after the resolution of this form of uncertainty. Brugiavini shows that consumers purchase insurance against their own survival probability type at a young age and then "do not undertake further transactions" (p. 31). In this model, it is better to buy the annuity early in life before you—and the insurance company—learn about your health classification. These sorts of models assume that you can borrow and lend at the same riskless rate during the entire life cycle. Although this assumption might be somewhat unrealistic in practice, the important insight from Brugiavini's model is the optimality of buying annuities before the insurance company suspects you are anti-selecting.

In contrast to this "buy them early" result, Yagi and Nishigaki (1993) focused on the consumption aspect of annuities. In particular, they derived the demand function for the annuities in the case in which the capital market is imperfect and life annuities must be locked in for life and (usually) pay out a fixed or constant income throughout the retirement period. They then proved that "the individual holds assets not only in the form of actuarial notes, but also in the form of monetary wealth" (p. 385). In other words, less than 100% is allocated to life annuities—in contrast to the Yaari (1965) result—because of the irreversibility of annuities and the inability to roll over differing amounts of actuarial notes.

On the topic of self-annuitization and the ability to beat the return from the life annuity, a number of related research articles can be found. Khorasanee (1996) considered two ways for a retiree to obtain a pension from a retirement fund. The first is through the purchase of a life annuity providing a level monetary income, and the second is through the withdrawal of income from a fund invested in equities. He used deterministic and stochastic models to assess the risks and benefits associated with each approach. In each case, the projected cash flows were compared with those from a whole life annuity providing an income linked to price inflation. He concluded that

although each of the two options considered involves significant risks, each method may be attractive to certain groups of pensioners, particularly those with additional savings held outside the retirement fund. (p. 229)

Milevsky (1998) examined the do-it-yourself option and arrived at the following conclusion: "In the current environment, a sixty-five-year-old female (male) has a ninety percent (eighty-five percent) chance of beating the rate of return from a life annuity, until age eighty" (p. 401).

The product allocation dimension was addressed by Kapur and Orszag (1999). They derived the optimal investment decisions of an individual who retires with a given level of assets and decides to invest in annuities and equities to provide income in retirement. They found that the optimal portfolio decision depends on risk aversion but, optimally, all individuals switch to annuities as they age. Also, continuing to focus on the idea of an optimal annuitization date, they found that the risk-adjusted losses from early annuitization can be significant.

Campbell, Cocco, Gomes, and Maenhout (2001) built a partial equilibrium life-cycle model calibrated to population parameters. They observed a welfare gain equivalent to 3.7% of consumption from the investment of half of retirement wealth into equities accompanied by a reduction in the U.S. Social Security payroll tax rate to maintain the same average replacement rate of income in retirement. In Cocco, Gomes, and Maenhout (2005), they solved a realistically calibrated life-cycle model of consumption and portfolio choice with nontradable labor income and borrowing constraints. They then showed that a crucial determinant of borrowing capacity and portfolio allocation is the lower bound for the income distribution. Essentially, both of these studies "prove" that life annuities offered by a social security system enable consumers to take on more financial risk than otherwise early in life. And although this finding might seem intuitive or just plain obvious, it is comforting to see that these insights can be embedded in a dynamic life-cycle model of savings and consumption.

When self-annuitization is considered, the equity risk premium may exceed the mortality credits—if only fixed annuities are available—but shortfall is always a risk. This possibility was stressed in Albrecht and Maurer (2002). They wrote:

> In comparison to private annuity products a self-annuitization strategy using mutual fund withdrawal plans contains, in particular for high entry ages, a substantial risk of outliving the individual's wealth, as long as the benchmark (the annuity) is based on a competitive investment return. (p. 284)

In terms of the optimal allocation in a VIA, Charupat and Milevsky (2002) showed that for constant relative risk aversion (CRRA) preferences and geometric Brownian motion dynamics, the optimal asset allocation during the annuity decumulation (payout) phase is identical to that for the accumulation (savings) phase. This finding is the classical Merton (1971) solution.

Blake, Cairns, and Dowd (2003) considered the choices available to a member of a defined contribution (DC) pension plan at the time of retirement for conversion of his or her pension fund into a stream of retirement income. Their results suggest that the best distribution plan does not usually involve a bequest but rather pays regular mortality credits to the plan member in return for the residual fund reverting to the insurance company on the plan member's death. In other words, the best distribution plan is one in which more consumption during life is traded for zero consumption at death. Such a product is, of course, a life annuity with no period certain (PC) or death benefit. But these authors did find that utility and welfare gains depend on the plan member's attitude toward risk. For highly risk-averse retirees, the appropriate plan is a conventional life annuity. If the retiree has a stronger appetite for risk, however, the optimal plan involves a mix of bonds and equities, with the optimal mix depending on the plan member's degree of risk aversion. Importantly, they found that "the optimal age to annuitize depends on the bequest utility and the investment performance of the fund during retirement" (p. 29). Once again, the researchers decide there is an optimal age that depends on both personal preferences and economic variables.

This line of research was pursued by a number of researchers. For example, Dushi and Webb (2004) used numerical optimization techniques to conclude that it is optimal for couples to delay annuitization until they are aged 73–82 and, in some cases, never to annuitize. For single men and women, annuitizing at substantially younger ages, between 65 and 70, is usually optimal. Households that annuitize will generally wish to annuitize only part of their wealth.

Similarly, Gerrard, Haberman, and Vigna (2004) investigated the income drawdown option and, looking for optimal investment strategies to be adopted after retirement, allowed for periodic fixed withdrawals from the fund. Their main conclusion is that "for a pensioner with a not too high risk aversion, the income drawdown option should be preferred to immediate annuitization, adopting optimal investment strategies with a sufficiently good risky asset" (p. 341).

One of the first normative *product allocation* models—one that actually offered advice—involving annuities was developed in Chen and Milevsky (2003). They offered a sort of separation theorem:

> The first step of a well-balanced retirement plan is to locate a suitable mix of risky and risk-free assets independently of their mortality contingent status. Then, once a comfortable balance has been struck between risk and return, the annuitization decision should be viewed as a second-step "overlay" that is placed on top of the existing asset mix. And, depending on the strength of bequest motives and subjective health assessments, the optimal annuitized fraction will follow. (p. 71)

Although the Chen and Milevsky (2003) "separation" result is certainly valid under the hypothetical conditions specified in their assumptions, you could make an argument that once a life annuity is purchased and longevity risk is hedged, the investor can afford to take on more investment risk. In other words, the asset allocation can be tilted toward equity instead of bonds. In fact, a paper by Milevsky and Kyrychenko (2008) indicated that in the context of variable annuities, the presence of a life annuity put option does induce greater risk taking in practice. The individuals who have more longevity insurance within their variable annuities actually take on more investment risk.

In a fundamental extension and generalization of the classic Yaari (1965) paper, Davidoff, Brown, and Diamond (2005) examined demand for life annuities with market incompleteness. They found that some annuitization remains optimal over a wide range of preference parameters but complete annuitization does not. They also argued that utility need not satisfy the Von Neumann–Morgenstern axioms and need not be additively separable for the Yaari (1965) result to hold. Furthermore, annuities need not be actuarially fair; they only must offer positive net premiums (i.e., mortality credits) over conventional assets.

In terms of the optimal timing of annuitization, Kingston and Thorp (2005) wrote:

> The desire to keep consumption above a specified floor creates an incentive to annuitize earlier than otherwise. HARA (hyperbolic absolute risk aversion) agents must maintain an escrow fund in the risk-free asset to cover future subsistence, effectively shrinking the potential for wealth creation through risky asset investment compared with CRRA (constant relative risk aversion) agents, and making actuarially fair annuities more attractive. Secondly, divergence between a retiree's subjective assessment of their survival prospects and the annuity provider's objective assessment of their prospects will still add to any delay. (p. 239)

A similar life-cycle approach was taken by Cairns, Blake, and Dowd (2006), whose objective was to find the optimal dynamic asset allocation strategy for a DC pension plan that takes into account the stochastic features of the plan member's lifetime salary progression and the stochastic properties of the assets held in the pensioner's accumulating pension fund. Shi (2008) showed that in a DC plan, the freedom to optimally choose the annuitization time can lead to an increase of certainty-equivalent wealth of up to 1.8%. Thus, according to Shi, "The embedded annuitization option in the retirement option value is of significant economic value to individuals" (p. 29).

In a comprehensive life-cycle model similar to that of Cairns et al. (2006), Chen, Ibbotson, Milevsky, and Zhu (2006) developed a unified human capital–based framework to help individual investors with life insurance and asset allocation decisions. The model provides several key results, including the fact that investors need to make asset allocation decisions and life insurance decisions jointly. In an expanded book by the same authors (Ibbotson, Milevsky, Chen, and Zhu 2007), the authors showed how to integrate the entire personal balance sheet into individual investors' asset allocations through a systematic joint analysis of (1) how much life insurance a family needs to protect human capital and (2) how to allocate the family's financial capital. They proposed a life-cycle model that addresses the transition from the accumulation phase to the saving phase and the role of immediate payout annuities. In the same vein and spirit, Kaplan (2006) used simulation-based techniques to derive optimal allocations to annuities.

Optimal Timing and the Option to Wait. Milevsky and Young (2007a) were one of the first research teams to tackle the optimal timing of annuitization within the framework of optimal stopping and stochastic control. They motivated their paper by arguing: "Due to adverse selection, acquiring a lifetime payout annuity is an irreversible transaction that creates an incentive to delay" (p. 3138). They then differentiated between all-or-nothing situations and gradual situations. For the institutional all-or-nothing arrangement, in which annuitization must take place at one distinct point in time (e.g., retirement), they derived the optimal age at which to annuitize—namely, the age at which the option to delay has zero time value. Then, for the more general open-market structure, in which individuals can annuitize any fraction of their wealth at any time, they located a general optimal annuity-purchasing policy.

Their main conclusion is that an individual will initially annuitize a lump sum and then buy additional annuities slowly. The idea of slow annuitization, or a dollar-cost-averaging strategy, is also advocated and demonstrated in various simulation-based studies, such as Soares and Warshawsky (2004). Milevsky and Young (2007b) used preference-free dominance arguments to develop a framework for locating the optimal age (time) at which a retiree should purchase an irreversible life annuity. In this framework, the selection of time is a function of current annuity prices and mortality tables. Then, using the institutional characteristics of annuity markets in the United States, Milevsky and Young showed that annuitization prior to age 65 or 70 is dominated by temporary self-annuitization even in the absence of any bequest motives.

Along the same lines, but in a paper written for a more mathematical audience, Stabile (2006) examined the optimal annuitization time and the optimal consumption/investment strategies for a retired individual subject to a constant force of mortality in an all-or-nothing framework. The author showed that if the individual evaluates the consumption flow and the annuity payment stream in the same way, then, depending on the parameters of the economy, the annuity is purchased at retirement or never. The book by Sheshinski (2008) offers readers a theoretical analysis of the functioning of private annuity markets in a life-cycle model; the demand function for annuities is derived, and various macroeconomic implications are examined. In a follow-up paper, Sheshinski (2010) examined the implications of annuity timing and investigated some embedded options and options that offer partial refunds in certain states of nature.

In a closely related paper written for a practitioner audience, Goodman and Heller (2006) offered some caveats about the advice of delaying annuitization. They wrote: "If one tries to self-annuitize and draw down the same level of income as payable under a life annuity, there will be more than a 50% chance that he or she will run of out of funds while still alive" (p. 9). In other words, the risk is substantial. The authors concluded that only a life annuity, whether fixed or variable, provides the highest level of living income available to a retired individual. In terms of the timing of annuitization, they stated that, if no significant change in interest rates is expected, a 5-year delay from age 65 to age 70 results in about a 5% loss in future income. Furthermore, delaying the start of life annuity income from age 65 to age 75, a 10-year delay, can easily result in a 15% loss in future income. In their opinion, given the sharper increase in mortality rates after age 70, "it pays to begin life annuity income no later than at age 70" (p. 9).

Stevens (2009) examined the problem of systematic longevity risk, which is the probability that hazard rates across different individuals might not be independent, in which case the law of large numbers might lose effectiveness in diversifying mortality risk. For example, a cure for cancer might reduce mortality rates for the entire population, which would wreak havoc on such pricing models as the GAPM. He claimed that because of the uncertainty in the future prices of annuities, for an individual aged 65 to purchase an annuity currently, instead of postponing the annuity purchase, is utility increasing. This conclusion differs from much of the literature cited earlier. Stevens claimed that this conclusion results from systematic longevity risk. He found that it is optimal to purchase—at an earlier age than found in other researchers' results—an annuity with a short deferral period.

In other words, not everyone agrees that delaying annuitizing to age 75 or so is low risk. In yet another anti-delay advocacy piece, Dellinger (2011) argued: "To the extent one's objective is to maximize retirement income with the potential to keep pace with inflation while minimizing the probability of outliving that income, delaying income annuity purchase can be suboptimal" (p. 1).

So, most authors agree that annuitization at some advanced age is optimal—fully or partially—but researchers disagree about the exact age, given the loss of liquidity and irreversibility. Interestingly, according to Zeng (2010), the utility loss because of the irreversibility of a future life annuity purchase is small for the retiree.

Devolder and Hainaut (2006) found that optimal consumption may be split into two periods. During the first one, the budget constraint is inactive: "An individual old enough and without any bequest motive should dedicate a part of his wealth to purchase a life annuity" (p. 47). In a companion paper (Hainaut and Devolder 2006), the authors went further and argued, "An interesting observation is that optimal asset allocation still includes a life annuity if the retiree wishes to pass on a bequest to his relatives" (p. 631).

In the continuous-time finance literature, the paper by Pliska and Ye (2007) generalized the Yaari (1965) model to include risky assets, which is similar to the work by Richard (1975). They modeled the optimal insurance purchase and consumption under an uncertain lifetime for a wage earner in a simple economic environment, successfully obtaining explicit solutions in the case of CRRA utility. In a similar framework, Gupta and Li (2007) found that high insurance charges can make the net return from the annuity less than the return from other available investment assets—for example, the risk-free asset. A related paper by Goda and Ramsay (2007) examined the optimal guarantee—such as a PC in a life annuity—and showed, on the one hand, that if the retiree's bequest constant—which is the strength of retiree's utility of bequest, or the minimum inheritance he or she would like to leave to heirs—is less than or equal to the lower bequest threshold, then a straight life annuity without the guarantee period is optimal. On the other hand, if the retiree's bequest constant is greater than or equal to the upper bequest threshold, then the maximum guarantee period is the best. Once again, the intuition here is that if you want to leave something for the kids, make sure to select a long PC.

A slightly different perspective on the important role of life annuities in the optimal portfolio is offered by Babbel and Merrill (2007a). They wrote:

> By covering at least basic expenses with lifetime income annuities, retirees are able to focus on discretionary funds as a source for enjoyment. Locking in basic expenses also means that the retiree's discretionary funds can remain invested in equities for a longer period of time, bringing the benefits of historically higher returns that can stretch the useful life of those funds even further. The key in all of this is to begin by covering all of the basic living expenses with lifetime income annuities. Then, to provide for additional desirable consumption levels, you will want to annuitize a portion of the remainder of your assets while making provisions for extra emergency expenses and, if desired, a bequest. (p. 11)

Babbel and Merrill (2007a) provided strong advocacy for the role of life annuities, and Babbel (2008) stressed the importance of life annuities for females, who risk even lower standards of living than males in the absence of such annuities. In yet another endorsement, according to Freedman (2008), life annuities can be used to extend the left-hand (low-risk) side of the efficient frontier. Reichenstein (2003), in a practitioner-oriented article, discussed the pros and cons of annuitizing a portion of the retirement portfolio and presented the by-now-familiar trade-off between reducing longevity risk and reducing the amount of wealth available to beneficiaries. This issue is the single most important trade-off involved in the decision to annuitize.

Horneff, with various co-authors, has written a series of papers geared toward an academic audience on the optimal allocation and timing of annuitization: Horneff, Maurer, Mitchell, and Dus (2008); Horneff, Maurer, Mitchell, and Stamos (2009); Horneff, Maurer, and Stamos (2008); Horneff, Maurer, Mitchell, and Stamos (2010); and Horneff, Maurer, and Rogalla (2010). In all of these papers, the authors used a utility-based framework to measure the welfare gains from allowing a robust and differing set of dynamic allocation strategies, including VIAs. The results, as I see them, are that the optimal strategy is to purchase annuities during your working life and continue to shift wealth into annuities well into retirement and until the age of 80 or 85. The authors stated: "The investor who moves her money out of liquid saving into survival-contingent assets gradually from middle age to retirement and beyond, will enhance her welfare by as much as 50%" (Horneff, Maurer, Mitchell, and Stamos 2009, p. 1688). The more relevant point is that they found VIAs to have an important role to play in the optimal portfolio.

Recently, Kartashov, Maurer, Mitchell, and Rogalla (2011) used the same techniques to examine variable investment-linked deferred annuities, which offer both an investment element (in terms of a mutual fund–style subaccount) and an insurance element (in terms of pooling longevity risks across the retiree group). An earlier article offering similar suggestions about the role of variable immediate—as well as real annuities—is Brown, Mitchell, and Poterba (2001).

Some research articles refer to annuities as (personal) longevity bonds and then derive the demand conditions. An example is Menoncin (2008), who demonstrated that the wealth invested in the longevity bond should be taken from the ordinary bond and the riskless asset proportionally to the duration of the two bonds. In other words, the funds to purchase a life annuity should be obtained from the fixed-income portion of the investor's portfolio.

As an alternative to annuitization, some researchers have proposed using alternative investments, such as real-return inflation-linked bonds. An example of this research is Shankar (2009), who proposed using Treasury Inflation-Protected Securities (TIPS) and longevity insurance—also known as deferred income annuities (DIAs) in some articles and as advanced life delayed annuities (ALDAs) in others—that would guarantee real annual withdrawal rates in excess of 5%

without any risk of financial ruin. His strategy involves investing the retirement savings in a combination of inflation-protected securities and longevity insurance that would generate a predetermined, inflation-protected lifetime income stream.

Sexauer, Peskin, and Cassidy (2012) proposed a decumulation benchmark comprising a laddered portfolio of TIPS for the first 20 years (consuming 88% of available capital) and a deferred life annuity purchased with the remaining 12%. This portfolio could be used directly by the investor (akin to indexing) or as a benchmark for evaluating the performance of a more aggressive strategy. One of the motivating reasons for the "TIPS over annuity" suggestion in the first 20 years of retirement is the concern about inflation risk that real-return bonds can address; other concerns include credit risk and the limited benefit of mortality credits at younger ages (ages 65–85). In a follow-up article, Sexauer and Siegel (2013) used the TIPS-plus-ALDA portfolio as the (almost) riskless asset, or base case, in an overall financial planning framework that spelled out, in language accessible to plan sponsors and human resource officers, how (given wide flexibility in the savings rate) to accumulate a desired level of guaranteed income for life.

In the product allocation literature, Pang and Warshawsky (2009), in comparing wealth management strategies for individuals in retirement, focused on trade-offs regarding wealth creation and income security. They examined a variety of strategies in a systematic and comprehensive manner. In a follow-up paper, Pang and Warshawsky (2010) derived optimal equity/bond/annuity portfolios for retired households that face stochastic capital market returns, differential exposures to mortality risk, uncertain uninsured health expenses, and differential social security and defined benefit (DB) pension coverage. In both Pang and Warshawsky papers (2009, 2010), annuities play an important role in the preferred strategies. Similarly, Koijen, Nijman, and Werker (2011) studied the life-cycle consumption and portfolio choice problem while taking into account annuity risk at retirement, and they also concluded that ignoring annuity risk before and at retirement can be "economically costly" (p. 799).

Park (2011) used simulation techniques to examine how immediate and deferred (longevity) annuities can affect probable income; he also took into account long-term care risk. His results indicate that for a male retiring at age 65 and facing investment and longevity risk who desires a 90% chance of adequate retirement income with an immediate annuity could optimally achieve that target by fully annuitizing his initial retirement wealth regardless of different equity allocations in his portfolio. If this retiree is assumed to be facing investment, longevity, and long-term care risk, however, he would need to annuitize 80–90% (not 100%) of his initial retirement wealth; some portion of his initial retirement wealth would have to be reserved to finance unexpected long-term care costs. This finding highlights a reason (and reminder) to keep some liquid assets.

Continuing with the theme of health care risk, which life annuities have difficulty addressing, Yogo (2011) developed a life-cycle model in which a household faces stochastic health depreciation and must choose consumption, health expenditure, and the allocation of its wealth between bonds, stocks, and housing. The author calibrated a model to U.S. population data and showed that the welfare gain from relaxing borrowing constraints on home equity is 5% of wealth at age 65. Similarly, the welfare gain from private annuitization is 16% of wealth at age 65. Similarly, Peijnenburg, Nijman, and Werker (2012) found that the timing of health cost risk is important. If out-of-pocket medical expenses can already be sizable early in retirement, empirically observed low annuitization levels are optimal. If health cost risk early in retirement is low, individuals would do better to save out of their annuity income to build a buffer for health cost shocks at later ages.

The technical problem of when to annuitize or begin withdrawals from a life annuity is intricately tied to the optimal timing of social security benefits. Sun and Webb (2011) used the similarity to argue "that the optimal claim age is between 67 and 70" (p. 907). They then used similar life-cycle models to calculate that the amount by which benefits payable at suboptimal ages must be increased so that a household is indifferent between claiming at those ages and the optimal combination of ages can be as high as 19.0%.

In a recent contribution to the optimal timing literature, Di Giacinto and Vigna (2012) proved that compulsory immediate annuitization is suboptimal and the cost varies, depending on the risk aversion of the member, in relative terms between 6% and 40% of initial wealth. This paper—like a number of others cited—supports making programmed withdrawals available as an option to DC plan participants.

In an interesting paper that touches on the cost of illiquidity, Wang and Young (2012) examined a world in which life annuities are cashable (that is, they can be sold back to the issuer at fair market value). In such a model, irreversibility is no longer a concern. They solved for the optimal investment strategy, optimal annuity purchase, and surrender strategies in this world. The paper is technical and based on some hard-to-justify assumptions, but the findings are interesting and thought provoking. They found that in such a model, individuals do annuitize more—no surprise—but actually surrender (or cash in) in various circumstances. Like many of the papers mentioned, these results are intuitive—perhaps even obvious if we consider that people are willing to pay for something they are likely to use. The authors' contribution to the literature is the ability to build a formal model that can actually price these options.

Finally, in a paper that raises some doubt about the appropriate model for dynamic life-cycle models of portfolio choice, including annuities, Charupat, Kamstra, and Milevsky (2012) wrote:

> Prices adjust gradually and over a period of several weeks and often months, in response to certain—and not necessarily riskless—interest rate changes. In particular, we find that changes to the 30-year U.S. mortgage rate provide a better fit and indication of where annuity payouts are headed, compared to the 10-year swap rate, for example. In addition, we find that the sensitivity to interest rate changes (that is, annuity duration) is asymmetric. Annuity prices react more rapidly and with greater sensitivity to an increase in the relevant interest rate compared to a decrease. (p. 1)

In conclusion, more than 50 articles discuss the optimal timing of annuitization, and although authors, papers, and models provide different conclusions, the main result seems to be that at some advanced age—perhaps as early as 60 or as late as 80—most consumers should have some of their wealth in life annuities.

Defining and Solving the Annuity Puzzle

Given the overwhelming evidence in favor of annuitization documented in the previous section, the reader may be surprised that so few individuals actively purchase life annuities or purchase as few as they do. As I have pointed out, the size of the voluntary life market is tiny relative to the much larger VA and mutual fund market. The question is, why? It has been labeled the "annuity puzzle" in the scholarly literature.

In my opinion, the first person to label this question as a formal puzzle, or at least to puzzle over it, was Huebner (1927). In his book on insurance economics, he wrote:

> The prospect, amounting almost to a terror, of living too long makes necessary the keeping of the entire principal intact to the end, so that as a final wind-up, the savings of a lifetime, which the owner does not dare to enjoy, will pass as an inheritance to others. In view of these facts, it is surprising that so few have undertaken to enjoy without fear the fruits of the limited competency they have succeeded in accumulating. This can be done only through annuities ... Why exist on $600, assuming 3% interest on $20,000, and then live in fear, when $1,600 may be obtained annually at age 65, through an annuity for all of life and minus all the fear ... (p. 189)

To most researchers in this field, the annuity puzzle is more closely associated with Modigliani (1986). In his Nobel Prize acceptance speech, he stated: "It is a well-known fact that annuity contracts, other than in the form of group insurance through pension systems, are extremely rare. Why this should be so is a subject of considerable current interest. It is still ill-understood" (p. 307).

The subsequent 25 years of scholarly literature have (1) attempted to solve the puzzle, (2) made the puzzle even worse, or (3) claimed that the puzzle does not exist. So, the literature is contradictory, but nevertheless, it is vast, and growing. What follows are the key articles in this area.

Williams (1986) blamed high interest rates:

> High interest rates decrease the demand for life annuities even if the potential annuitant does not believe that he or she could earn higher interest rates than the pension administrator or individual life insurer uses to calculate the lifetime income. Longer life expectances may also reduce the demand for annuities, but their impact is weaker than the effect of higher interest rates. If, as many persons believe, interest rates are not likely to return to earlier lower levels in the near future, one would expect an increase in the demand at retirement for lump sums under pension plans, individual deferred annuities, and supplementary life insurance contracts. (p. 169)

Friedman and Warshawsky (1990) blamed the high loads and costs embedded in annuities:

> An explanation for this phenomenon is based either on the actuarially unfair cost of annuities, importantly including the cost element arising from adverse selection, or on the interaction of the unfair annuity cost and an intentional bequest motive. (p. 152)

Bernheim (1991) blamed government social security:

> I find that social security annuity benefits significantly raise life insurance holdings and depress private annuity holdings among elderly individuals. These patterns indicate that the typical household would choose to maintain a positive fraction of its resources in bequeathable forms, even if insurance markets were perfect. (p. 899)

Brown and Poterba (2000) blamed marriage:

> The utility gain from annuitization is smaller for couples than for single individuals. Because most potential annuity buyers are married, this finding may help to explain the limited size of the market for single premium annuities in the United States. (p. 527)

Post, Gründl, and Schmeiser (2006) confirmed and reinforced the idea that family risk sharing and the high loads on annuities are jointly to blame for low levels of annuitization. Others have suggested that, although blaming bequests and the desire for legacy might seem natural—because the annuity is irreversible—these reasons might not be legitimate reasons for avoiding life annuities. Brown (2001) wrote: "There is no evidence that bequest motives are an important factor in making marginal annuity decisions" (p. 29).

Vidal-Meliá and Lejárraga-García (2006) concluded that few couples would be willing to purchase life annuities once they had taken into account the combined effects of market imperfections, the possibility of preexisting annuities, and the bequest motive. Mottola and Utkus (2007) echoed these ideas:

> It seems clear that there is a strong desire for married couples to de-annuitize with many actively trying, by selecting products, to overcome the federally mandated default of a joint-and-survivor annuity. (p. 8)

Purcal and Piggott (2008) wrote: "Results suggest that the bequest motive is the strongest single deterrent to annuity purchase, followed by social security" (p. 513).

Lockwood (2012) argued:

> People with plausible bequest motives are likely to be better off not annuitizing any wealth at available rates. The evidence suggests that bequest motives play a central role in limiting the demand for annuities. (p. 226)

Pashchenko (2010) examined a variety of explanations for low levels of annuitization—most of them alluded to here—but then concluded, "Among the traditional explanations, pre-annuitized wealth has the largest quantitative contribution to the annuity puzzle" (p. 1).

Dushi and Webb (2004) continued with the idea of preannuitized wealth. Using data from the Assets and Health Dynamics among the Oldest Old and Health and Retirement Study panels, they concluded that "much of the failure of the average currently retired household to annuitize can be attributed to the exceptionally high proportions of the wealth of these cohorts that is pre-annuitized" (p. 109). In other words, the preannuitized have too many annuities already in the form of pensions and social security.

Bütler, Peijnenburg, and Staubli (2011) wrote:

> Most industrialized countries provide a subsistence level consumption floor in old age, usually in the form of means-tested benefits or income supplements. The availability of such means-tested payments creates an incentive to cash out (occupational) pension wealth for low and middle income earners, instead of taking the annuity. (p. 1)

In an interesting forecast of future prospects for this market, Dushi and Webb (2004) concluded: "We expect younger cohorts to have smaller proportions of pre-annuitized wealth and project increasing demand for annuitization as successive cohorts age" (p. 109). McCarthy and Mitchell (2004), coming to similar conclusions, wrote that "the demand for annuities is likely to rise in the future, driven by increased longevity, diminished public and corporate pensions, and the availability of new annuity linked products" (p. 43).

Sinclair and Smetters (2004) argued that uncertain health expenditures are to blame for the annuity puzzle. They wrote:

Individuals face a risk of health shocks which simultaneously cause large uninsured expenses and shorten the life expectancy. The value of a life annuity then decreases at the same time as the need for cash increases, undermining its effectiveness in providing financial security. When the risk of such a health shock is substantial, it is no longer optimal for risk-averse individuals with uncertain lifespans to hold all of their wealth in life annuity form, even if annuity contracts are reversible, and bequest motives, transaction costs, and adverse selection are absent. (p. 1)

Ameriks, Caplin, Laufer, and Van Nieuwerburgh (2011) also focused attention on the importance of long-term care and medical risk. They wrote that "demand for annuities would be far higher if they included some acceptable form of long-term care insurance" (p. 520).

Not all countries experience the same low levels of voluntary annuitization as found in the United States and Canada. In Chile, for example, a large number of retirees purchase additional annuities. James, Martinez, and Iglesias (2006) documented that almost two-thirds of all retirees have annuitized, which is a high proportion compared with other countries. The authors argued that the high rate of annuitization in Chile is the result of guarantees and regulations that constrain payout choices, insure retirees through the minimum pension guarantee, eliminate other DB components, and give a competitive advantage to insurance companies selling annuities.

For Switzerland, which offers a robust dataset for studying annuitization, Bütler and Teppa (2007) empirically examined the levels of annuitization in DB pension plans. They concluded that low accumulation of retirement assets is strongly associated with the choice of the lump sum because of the availability of means-tested social assistance. They further claimed that the sponsor's default option is highly influential in the decision to annuitize.

Also writing about the Swiss annuity system, Avanzi (2010) claimed that higher annuitization is observed because

these [factors] include annuitisation as a default choice, a high level of regulation that fosters trust from the insured, a legal guarantee of benefits, the absence of market risk borne by the insured, a favorable tax structure, substantial savings with flexible withdrawal options, home ownership, generosity of benefits, as well as additional elements. (p. 155)

Continuing with the case of Switzerland, Bütler, Staubli, and Zito (forthcoming) noted that in 2004, several Swiss insurance companies reduced the conversion rate from wealth to income, which means that annuity factors increased and the cost of guaranteed lifetime income increased. The authors found that, as a consequence of the policy change, the fraction of individuals choosing an annuity decreased by 16.8 percentage points.

Ganegoda and Bateman (2008) suggested that the thin and fading market for life annuities in Australia might be the result of a "lack of consumer awareness of the risks of not annuitizing" (p. 1).

In the United Kingdom, Inkmann, Lopes, and Michaelides (2011) set out to

> provide an in-depth empirical analysis of the characteristics of households that participate (or not) in the U.K. voluntary annuity market. We document that annuity demand increases . . . [as] financial wealth, education, and life expectancy [increase], while it decreases [with increases] in pension income and a possible bequest motive for surviving spouses. (p. 315)

In Italy, Cappelletti, Guazzarotti, and Tommasino (2011) found "a strong demand for annuity products, at least with respect to the one that we observe today, at current market prices" (p. 18).

One thing is for certain: There are substantial differences in annuitization rates across countries and even within countries by various demographic and socioeconomic groups. In an interesting experiment involving the U.S. military, Warner and Pleeter (2001) studied a U.S. government program that offered to more than 65,000 enlisted members separating from the military (separatees) the choice between an annuity and a lump-sum payment. Despite having been offered breakeven discount rates exceeding 17%, most of the separatees selected the lump sum, not the annuity. According to the authors, this (irrationality) saved U.S. taxpayers $1.7 billion in costs because the annuity was a much better deal.

In recent attempts to salvage the rational model, some have conjectured that default and credit risk, rather than behavioral or bequest factors, might be to blame for the annuity puzzle. For example, Jang, Koo, and Lee (2010) claimed that "fear of the default risk of annuity providers may have hampered growth of annuity markets" (p. 2). But using an equally sophisticated model, Lopes and Michaelides (2007) suggested otherwise. Their model calculations suggest that "a rare event [default] is unlikely to be the main explanation of the annuity market participation puzzle" (p. 84). Schulze and Post (2010) introduced an actuarial element to the discussion of the annuitization puzzle. In their models, "consideration of aggregate mortality risk may alleviate, but also intensify, the annuity puzzle" (p. 423).

Yaari without Strong Assumptions. In a widely cited, comprehensive, and influential paper, Davidoff, Brown, and Diamond (2005) argued:

> While incomplete annuity markets may render annuitization of a large fraction of wealth suboptimal, our simulation results show that this is not the case even in a habit-based model that intentionally leads to a severe mismatch between desired consumption and the single payout trajectory provided by an incomplete annuity market. These results suggest that lack of annuity demand may arise from behavioral considerations, and that some mandatory annuitization may be welfare increasing. It also suggests the importance of behavioral modeling of annuity demand to understand the equilibrium offerings of annuity assets. (p. 1589)

In other words, the culprit is behavioral.

This approach is echoed by Hurd, Panis, Smith, and Zissimopoulos (2004). After extensive simulations based on the life-cycle model, they concluded that "we need a new understanding of the motives for the lack of annuitization, and possibly, a new theoretical structure" (p. 130). In a further reinforcement of the puzzle, Chalmers and Reuter (2012), after examining the choice between life annuities and lump sums made by 32,000 retiring public employees in the United States, found little evidence that retiree "demand for life annuities rises when life annuity prices fall" (p. 1). In other words, even when life annuities go "on sale," consumers do not seem interested in them. In one of the final nails into the rational coffin, Chalmers and Reuter found "strong evidence that demand responds to recent equity returns" (p. 1). Thus, when stock markets have gone up in the past few months, the demand for annuities declines, and vice versa. Previtero (2011) presented evidence from corporate (IBM) pension plan behavior that is consistent with employees extrapolating from recent stock market returns. He argued that this myopic extrapolation can result in a significant reduction in retirement wealth if, for example, individuals annuitize too early because of a market drop.

The Behavioral Angle. So, many recent researchers have been taking the behavioral angle. For example, Hu and Scott (2007) claimed: "Mental accounting and loss aversion can explain the unpopularity of annuities by framing them as risky gambles where potential losses loom larger than potential gains" (p. 71). Brown, Kling, Mullainathan, and Wrobel (2008) wrote, in an important paper about the impact of framing, that

> framing matters for annuitization decisions: In a consumption frame, annuities are viewed as valuable insurance, whereas in an investment frame, the annuity is a risky asset because the payoff depends on an uncertain date of death. Survey evidence is consistent with our hypothesis that framing matters: The vast majority of individuals prefer an annuity over alternative products when presented in a consumption frame, whereas the majority of

individuals prefer non-annuitized products when presented in an investment frame. To the extent that the investment frame is the dominant frame for consumers making financial planning decisions for retirement, this finding may help to explain why so few individuals annuitize. (p. 308)

Continuing the exact same reasoning, Brown (2009) wrote that "part of the answer to why consumers are so reluctant to annuitize will probably be found through a more rigorous study of the various psychological biases that individuals bring to the annuity decision" (p. 1).

Bütler and Staubli (2011) wrote that "annuity payout choices are significantly influenced by default options and peer effects" (p. 195).

Drilling down into the behavioral explanations, Gazzale and Walker (2009) offered two plausible behavioral biases:

Our first hypothesis is a risk-ordering bias: retirees effectively overweight the early risk (an early death) relative to the later risk (a longer-than-anticipated retirement). Our second hypothesis is an endowment effect stemming from loss aversion. (p. 21)

They went on to find support for these hypotheses in a laboratory setting capturing many of the salient aspects of the annuity decision.

Also in the realm of behavioral explanations, Panis (2004) conducted an extensive survey and found that

those with greater annuitization were more satisfied in retirement, and they maintained their satisfaction throughout retirement. By contrast, retirees without lifelong annuities have become somewhat less satisfied over the years. The guaranteed income benefits may reduce anxiety about the risks of outliving one's savings and ending up in poverty. (p. 13)

In a recent NBER paper, Beshears, Choi, Laibson, Madrian, and Zeldes (2012), reporting on a large-scale study in which individuals were given various hypothetical annuitization choices, found that "allowing individuals to annuitize a fraction of their wealth increases annuitization relative to a situation where annuitization is an all-or-nothing decision" (p. 1). Also, they emphasized the importance of framing. Moreover, although Beshears et al. (2012) and related studies, such as Brown et al. (2008), do not report on real choices by live people with actual money, presumably something can be gleaned from how people respond in surveys to different framing of the same economic situation. Indeed, most of the foundational studies in behavioral finance in the 1980s and 1990s were assembled from similar surveys, experiments, and hypotheticals.

Tax Treatment. Although not addressing the annuity puzzle directly, Brown et al. (1999) examined the tax treatment of nonqualified annuities in the United States and made a number of observations and suggestions to help improve the efficiency of the market.[33] They examined an alternative method of taxing annuities that would avoid changing the fraction of the annuity payment included in taxable income as the annuitant ages but would still raise the same expected present discounted value of revenues as the current income tax rule. They found "that a shift to a constant inclusion ratio increases the utility of annuitants and that this increase is greater for more risk averse individuals" (p. 563). For a discussion of income taxes in the United States and how they affect the relative appeal of annuities versus fully taxable assets, see Babbel and Reddy 2009.

Brown and Poterba (2006) examined specifically the market for tax-deferred variable annuities—which is much larger than the market for life annuities—and identified two factors that have contributed to its success and growth. The first is the opportunity for tax deferral, and the second is the insurance features of variable annuities. They also found that VA ownership strongly increases as income, wealth, age, and education increase.

Brunner and Pech (2008) offered a different perspective on the taxation of life annuities. Considering a nonlinear tax on annuity payoffs, they found that it can be used to correct the so-called distortion of the rate of return caused by asymmetrical information.

In some countries and markets, income taxes create an additional incentive (as opposed to barrier) to actual annuitization. Charupat and Milevsky (2001) documented an intriguing tax arbitrage opportunity involving the lighter tax treatment of life annuities in Canada. This opportunity might explain the (relatively) higher demand for life annuities in Canada, per capita, than in the U.S. market. But, of course, overall Canadian life annuity demand is still low relative to what might be expected from a life-cycle model.

Policy Prescriptions. Some analysts have moved from posing and solving the annuity puzzle to offering policy suggestions or prescriptions on how to increase annuitization rates. Teppa (2011) offered the following suggestion: "The annuitization puzzle may be alleviated by helping individuals in better assessing their perceived longevity risk, rather than forcing their actions" (p. 1). Direr (2010) suggested that "a minimal degree of flexibility could well promote wealth annuitization by reducing the mismatch between the desired consumption path and the annuity income stream" (p. 51). Scott, Watson, and Hu (2011) suggested product innovations as one way to increase participation in the market. They claimed that product innovation to concentrate on late-life payouts could improve participation. They wrote: "The most promising area for large increases in (mortality credits) is not lowering annuity costs but rather offering annuity products focused on late-life payouts" (p. 238). This approach (known as an ALDA in Milevsky

---

[33]For a discussion of income taxes in the United States and how they affect the relative appeal of annuities versus fully taxable assets, see Babbel and Reddy (2009).

2005a and DIA in industry jargon) was extensively analyzed and shown to provide value in a life-cycle model by Gong and Webb (2010). Webb (2011) offered similar policy suggestions.

Murray and Klugman (1990) suggested other innovations to improve annuitization:

> For older persons in relatively poor health, life annuities may not provide a sufficiently high expected return to justify their use . . . [but] a market should develop to provide underwritten life annuities to those with impaired health. (p. 50)

In other words, one solution to the annuity puzzle (low annuitization rates) would be to create an active market for impaired annuities sold to less healthy annuitants.

Murtaugh, Spillman, and Warshawsky (2001) claimed that combining immediate annuities with long-term disability insurance would reduce the cost of both and make them available to more individuals by reducing adverse selection in the income annuity portion and minimizing the need for medical underwriting for disability coverage. This approach is, implicitly, another suggestion for improving annuitization rates, but Davidoff (2009) questioned whether it would increase annuitization rates. His simulations indicate that life annuities and long-term care insurance might be substitutes rather than complements.

Creighton, Jin, Piggott, and Valdez (2005) analyzed the reasons for the "failure of longevity insurance markets" (p. 417) and examined possible innovations in both markets and public policy that might lead to a more vibrant market, including pooled annuities that resemble a type of tontine, described earlier. Mackenzie (2006) addressed the questions of whether annuitization or other restrictions on distributions should be mandatory and, if so, whether the provision of annuities should be privatized. Goldsticker (2007) proposed a mutual fund/tontine hybrid vehicle. It would be a pooled fund serving as a low-cost vehicle to provide annuity-like cash flows. Rotemberg (2009) proposed a new instrument to be called a "mutual inheritance fund," which would be another tontine-like innovation. Other innovative solutions that might help reduce the cost of providing life annuities, and thus spur demand, include the "pooled annuity fund" proposal made by Piggott, Valdez, and Detzel (2005) and by Bravo, Real, and da Silva (2009). The actuarial literature continues to produce interesting innovations in this area.

Agnew, Anderson, Gerlach, and Szykman (2008) focused on the important role of financial intermediaries and advisers in promoting and effecting annuitization. In experiments, they found that women are more likely than men to annuitize when offered actuarially fair annuities, which might be a further indication that framing is important.

©2013 The Research Foundation of CFA Institute

The report by Lieber (2010) and the report of the Council of Economic Advisers (2012) discussed efforts by the Obama administration to promote annuitization.

In a widely circulated proposal, Gale, Iwry, John, and Walker (2008) argued that retirees should be given an opportunity to "test drive" a lifetime income product, which would help retirees overcome existing biases, reframe their view of lifetime-income products, and improve their ability to evaluate their retirement distribution options. They proposed that a substantial portion of assets in 401(k)s and other similar plans be automatically directed (defaulted) into a two-year trial income product when retirees take distributions from their plans, unless they affirmatively choose not to participate. They wrote:

> Retirees would receive twenty-four consecutive monthly payments from the automatic trial income plan. At the end of the trial period, retirees may elect an alternative distribution option or, if they do nothing, be defaulted into a permanent income distribution plan. (p. 3)

This suggestion has similarities to other default options in DC plans, such as life-cycle funds and automatic savings plans.

Brown and Nijman (2011) offered similar suggestions, albeit to a Dutch audience. Specifically, they suggested that, instead of compulsory annuitization of all retirement wealth, individuals be required to annuitize a minimum amount in a reliably inflation-indexed annuity and that some additional amounts of annuitization be structured as automatic with an opt-out provision.

Many other suggestions continue to be provided by practitioners, policymakers, and scholars on how to innovate in this market.

Yet, not all scholars agree that policymakers should actively increase annuitization. Feigenbaum and Gahramanov (2012) used a sophisticated overlapping generations model to argue counterintuitively,

> If households were to begin following the advice of most economists to annuitize, there would be short-term gains as households enjoy higher returns on their savings. But later generations would be hurt as they stop receiving accidental bequests. In the long run, everyone would be worse off. So we would argue that policymakers should not implement measures intended to encourage annuitization. (p. 91)

In a similar paper using the rational life-cycle model with a more general aversion to uncertainty, Bommier and Le Grand (2012) suggested, "A possible reason for the low level of wealth annuitization may, therefore, simply be that individuals are too risk averse to purchase annuities" (p. 28).

For those interested in reading more in this "life annuities are not necessarily all good" literature, I suggest Fehr and Habermann (2008), who argued that although young cohorts experience significant welfare gains, future generations are hurt by lower bequest amounts. This is a different perspective, to say the least.[34]

I conclude the literature review of the annuity puzzle with a quote from recent article by Benartzi, Previtero, and Thaler (2011):

> The notion that consumers are simply not interested in annuities is clearly false. Social Security remains a wildly popular federal program, and those workers who still have defined benefit pension plans typically choose to retain the annuity rather than switch to a lump-sum distribution. Furthermore, when participants in defined benefit pension plans with built-in annuitized payout are offered the opportunity to switch to a defined contribution plan, most stick with what they have. The tiny market share of individual annuities should not be viewed as an indicator of underlying preferences but as a consequence of institutional factors about the availability and framing of annuity options. (p. 161)

In a private conversation I had with Yaari, he stated that perhaps one of the reasons many people did not appreciate the value of life annuities was that personal tastes and preferences can change over time and they know it. The current design of annuities might not allow retirees to adapt to changes in their own tastes. These changes might be in legacy preferences or even for spending more now versus later. One thing is certain, for those writing in 2012, the annuity puzzle is not as perplexing as it was 45 years ago.

The Money's Worth Ratio around the World

As I explained in Chapter 2, one of the most important formulas in the life annuity literature is the money's worth ratio (MWR), which compares the theoretical (fair) price of a life annuity with the actual market price. The higher the ratio, the better the value from the life annuity. The MWR metric has been used in many studies and across various countries. In this section, I will review and summarize the key articles in this literature.

To my knowledge, the first paper to use the MWR in the context of life annuities is Warshawsky (1988). He collected market annuity prices in the United States over a period of almost 70 years and concluded:

> Load factors on life annuities issued to 65-year-old males and females over the period 1919 through 1984 have ranged from 10 cents to 29 cents per dollar of actuarial present value. From 8 cents to 16 cents of these loads

---

[34]In a telling comment along the same lines, Davidoff mentioned to me in conversation that, precisely for this reason, the Davidoff, Brown, and Diamond (2005) *American Economic Review* paper, Diamond selected the title "Annuities and Individual Welfare," as opposed to using the words "consumer" or "society" welfare.

represents the cost of adverse selection, and approximately 7.5 cents represents transaction costs. The cost of adverse selection increased during the middle period of study, 1941–1962, on annuities sold to males, while the cost of adverse selection continually declined for females. (p. 518)

The main purpose in computing the MWR in Warshawsky and many other papers is to quantify the impact of adverse selection on the return from life annuities.

A similar study was conducted by Friedman and Warshawsky (1990), who concluded:

Expected yields offered on individual life annuities in the United States during 1968–1983 were lower on average by 4.21–6.13 percent per annum or 2.43–4.35 percent per annum after allowing for adverse selection, than yields on alternative long-term fixed-income investments. (p. 152)

In the same vein, Mitchell, Poterba, Warshawsky, and Brown (1999) conducted an extensive study of annuity prices in the United States and found that the average annuity policy available to a 65-year-old man in 1995 delivered payouts valued at between 80 cents and 85 cents per dollar of annuity premium. In other words, the MWR was much less than unity. They also found substantial heterogeneity among annuity providers in the payouts per dollar of premium payment and found that various companies offered prices that were quite different from the average. They concluded that in the late 1990s, "from the standpoint of potential purchasers, an individual annuity contract appears to be a more attractive product today than 10 years ago" (p. 1316). Poterba (2001) suggested: "Requiring all persons to annuitize their retirement account balances at a specified age is one way to reduce the degree of adverse selection in the annuity market substantially" (p. 268). This suggestion is consistent with Walliser (2000), who found that adverse selection caused by the fact that annuitization is optional in most countries and jurisdictions increases annuity prices by 7–10%.

In the U.S. market, Brown (2002) examined the impact on the MWR of different mortality rates for different socioeconomic groups. He found that during the payout phase of the annuity, mortality differences are also important: "The MWR is lower for men than for women and for blacks than for whites, and increases [with] an individual's education level" (p.437). An important conclusion from this paper is that if life annuities were mandatory and everyone paid the same price, there would be a substantial (exceeding 20%) transfer of wealth from the shorter-lived group to the longer-lived group. In related research, Carlson and Lord (1986) argued that any prohibition in the use of gender as an insurance classification parameter is indefensible, as it would also transfer wealth from shorter-lived groups (males) to longer-lived groups (females).

In a wide-ranging international comparison, James and Vittas (2001), from, respectively, the IMF and World Bank, examined the market pricing of annuities and came to similar conclusions as Mitchell et al. (1999) regarding the high value of annuities. They wrote:

> Preliminary findings suggest that the cost of annuities is lower than might be expected. When using the risk-free discount rate, MWRs of nominal annuities based on annuitant mortality tables exceed 97% and even when using population mortality tables they exceed 90%—neither the industry commissions nor the effects of adverse selection appear to be as large as anticipated. (p. i)

James and Song (2001), who conducted a similar international comparison, were careful to note that the MWR will depend on the particular assumptions used to value the theoretical annuity. They found that "when discounting at the risk-free rate, MWRs for annuitants are surprisingly high—greater than 95% in most countries and sometimes greater than 100%" (p. 1).

Recall that the theoretical price of a life annuity, which is the denominator of the MWR calculation, involves assumptions regarding both mortality and interest rates. The two effects are often difficult to disentangle in market prices. For example, Mitchell and McCarthy (2002), using data from the United Kingdom and the United States, claimed that

> the relatively lower mortality among older Americans who purchase annuities is equivalent to using a discount rate that is 50–100 bps below the U.K. rate for compulsory annuitants or 10–20 bps lower than the U.K. rate for voluntary annuitants. (p. 38)

Interestingly, James and Vittas (2001) did find that real (inflation-adjusted) annuities—available in Chile, Israel, and the United Kingdom and now available in the United States (but rarely purchased) from a limited number of insurance companies—have MWR values that are 7–9% lower than those of nominal annuities. (For an examination of the pension systems—including the role of annuities—in Australia, Chile, Denmark, Sweden, and Switzerland, see Rocha, Vittas, and Rudolph 2011.)

The U.K. market is by far the largest life annuity market (by volume of sales) in the world. Gunawardena, Hicks, and O'Neill (2008) showed that the pension annuities market tripled in size between 1992 and 2007. In 2007, premiums in the pension annuities market were more than £11 billion and more than 400,000 contracts were sold. Demand for pension annuities is set to rise further in the coming years because of a rise in the number of maturing DC pensions. Cannon and Tonks (2009) computed the MWR of annuities in the United Kingdom and found that, on average, the money's worth over the sample period for 65-year-old males was 90% and for 65-year-old females was similar but slightly higher, 91%. Taking into account load factors associated with annuity contracts and making a comparison with other financial and insurance products, this finding implies that annuities are fairly priced. Some evidence indicates, however, that money's worth has fallen since 2002. Cannon and Tonks (2008) is another excellent source of information about life annuities in general and the U.K. life annuity market in particular. For more about the U.K. market, see also Telford, Browne, Collinge, Fulcher, Johnson, Little, Lu, Nurse, Smith, and Zhang (2011).

Continuing with life annuities in the United Kingdom, Finkelstein and Poterba (2002, 2004) found substantial evidence of adverse selection and *ex post* mortality that was different for different socioeconomic levels and found that the "money's worth ratio increases with the length of the guarantee period" (p. 45). An interesting finding—which is consistent with James and Vittas (2001)—is that the MWR for an annuity product with a rising nominal payout stream or an inflation-indexed payout stream was lower than that for a level nominal product. The cause might be low demand, which reduces competition. Brown, Mitchell, and Poterba (2002) found the same and wrote that "the money's worth ratio of nominal annuities exceeds the money's worth of inflation-indexed annuities both in the United States and in other countries" (p. 24). Again, this phenomenon does not appear to be the case in Chile, which makes it difficult to generalize. According to James, Martinez, and Iglesias (2006), the MWR for indexed annuities in Chile is 98%. They suggest two reasons. First, in Chile, indexed financial instruments in which insurance companies can invest to hedge their risk are more widely available than in other countries. Second (and a more convincing reason, I believe), the forced indexation requirements eliminate adverse selection between nominal and real annuities.

For Australia, Ganegoda and Bateman (2008), using the MWR, found that annuities represent poor value for money. They found that the MWRs of Australian annuities are lower than international estimates and the total loadings are higher.

For Singapore, Fong, Mitchell, and Koh (2011) reported that the country's Central Provident Fund, a national DC pension scheme, has mandated annuitization of workers' retirement assets and, as a result, the government-offered annuities are estimated to provide MWRs exceeding unity.

Oddly enough—and consistent with the idea that each country and market is quite different and segmented—James and Sane (2003) found that in India, "unrealistically generous payouts with high money's worth ratios far exceeding 100 percent were offered until 2002." They reported that "one particular company reduced rates by much more than warranted, leading to a decline in MWRs to 90 percent, which was an increase in the load from less than nothing to more than 10 percent" (p. 258).

Indeed, the process by which a market develops for life annuities is interesting. The volume edited by Fornero and Luciano (2004), which includes some of the previously mentioned studies, examined the evolution of the European market in particular. The consensus appears to be that with the aging of the population and the transition from DB to DC pension plans, this trend will continue. This point is made by a variety of authors in the Fornero and Luciano volume and by Cannon and Tonks (2005) in the context of the United Kingdom.

Note that some notable problems arise when using the MWR for computing relative value and comparing markets and countries. This issue is emphasized (in the context of Singapore) by Fong, Lemaire, and Tse (2011), who wrote:

> It is necessary to consider the entire weighted distribution of annuity benefits, instead of focusing exclusively on its expected value, the numerator of the MWR metric. For instance, if the weighted discounted benefits are spread over a large range of values, the overall financial attractiveness of annuities may be less than what the MWR indicates. (p. 3)

This caveat is consistent with the evidence provided by Charupat, Kamstra, and Milevsky (2012) that market annuity prices take time (often months) to fully respond to changes in interest rates, which implies that a slice-in-time calculation of MWR might be comparing today's annuity price with yesterday's interest rate. See also Carson, Doran, and Dumm (2011), who examined market discipline in the individual annuity market by measuring annuity contract yields during the accumulation phase.

Finally, Rothschild (2009) looked back more than 200 years and examined one of the oldest known datasets for evidence of adverse selection. Using data from an 1808 Act of British Parliament that effectively opened a market for life annuities, he found (not surprisingly) that even back in 1808, healthier people purchased annuities and the less healthy and unhealthy stayed away from this market. For more information about annuities and tontines from the Middle Ages until the 20th century, the interested reader is referred to Jennings and Trout (1982), Ransom and Sutch (1987), and Jennings, Swanson, and Trout (1988). Given the widespread evidence over many centuries—offered by all of these authors—that healthier individuals are the ones who purchase annuities, Philipson and Becker (1998) made an interesting argument that, perhaps, when introducing mortality-contingent claims into a life-cycle model, longevity should be treated exogenously. Edwards (2012) provided more discussion of the economics of lifespan variation.

In a clever historical study, Salm (2011) used changes in pension laws for U.S. Union army veterans as a natural experiment to estimate the causal effect of pensions and life annuities on longevity. Examining the effects of the pension laws of 1907 and 1912, which granted old-age pensions to Union army veterans, he found that veteran pensions reduced mortality for both acute and nonacute causes of death. So, the endogeneity of income and longevity-contingent claims is not as farfetched as you might initially suspect. All of these findings echo the famous Jane Austen quote from *Sense and Sensibility* (published in 1811): "If you observe, people always live forever when there is an annuity to be paid them."

Other Institutional and Policy Literature

The final category in the life annuity literature is rather eclectic and a catchall for articles that do not fall neatly into any of the other five categories.

In terms of the history of annuity pricing, annuity use, and annuity popularity, I recommend the early article by Kopf (1927) and the more recent article by Lewin (2003). It is amazing how active the market for life annuities was in the 17th and 18th centuries and interesting how involved famous mathematicians and astronomers were in the development of pricing formulas. See, for example, the book by Bellhouse (2011) on the work of Abraham de Moivre and the work of Leonhard Euler—the first, a statistician, and the second, a mathematician of the first caliber—in the development of annuity pricing models. Poterba (2005) wrote:

> During a period of roughly three centuries, the major nation-states in Europe relied substantially on the sale of life annuity contracts to finance wars and other public expenditures. The nature of annuity products evolved during this time, from simple contracts that paid the same amount to all buyers, regardless of their age or gender, to more finely graded products that more closely resemble modern private insurance annuities. Leading mathematicians of this period contributed to important advances in the pricing of annuity contracts. The history of annuities also offers evidence of the role of sophisticated speculation by private sector investors . . . Syndicates arose to invest in annuity contracts when it was possible to profitably speculate against the governments that were selling them. (p. 207)

Moving to institutional and regulatory matters, and fast-forwarding to the twentieth century, Mehr (1958) discussed the regulation of VIAs and mused about the proper agency to oversee the sale and distribution of these products. The dilemma is whether to view them as securities or insurance or both. The VIA itself was created in the 1950s and is described at length in Biggs (1969) in the context of TIAA-CREF.

In the early 1990s, a number of researchers began viewing DB retirement pensions as a form of *longevity insurance*, which was a term not used by earlier researchers, such as Yaari (1965). First among them was Bodie (1990), who wrote that "defined benefit pensions offer the most complete type of retirement income insurance . . . [and] defined contribution pensions make sense as a supplement" (p. 30). Blake (1999) wrote that because DC plans do not offer longevity insurance, government has a role to play in helping develop and expand the life annuity market. Blake was one of the first to suggest that

> One key contribution of the government would be to supply long-term instruments such as indexed bonds and survivor bonds that would enable annuity providers to hedge risks that are beyond the resources and abilities of private sector organizations to hedge effectively and economically. (p. 367)

The market for longevity-linked bonds has spawned its own growing literature. MacMinn, Brockett, and Blake (2006) is an excellent starting point.

Munnell, Golub-Sass, Soto, and Vitagliano (2007) reviewed the major pension freezes during the period of 2005–2007 and explore the impact on employees at different stages in their careers. Four possible explanations are offered as to why employers are shutting down their plans: (1) to reduce workers' total compensation in the face of intense global competition; (2) to maintain existing compensation levels in the face of growing health benefit costs; (3) to avoid the market risk, longevity risk, and regulatory risk that make DB pensions unattractive to employers; and (4) to reflect the fact that traditional qualified pensions have become irrelevant to upper management, who now receive virtually all their retirement benefits through non-qualified plans. Whatever the reason, one thing is certain: As documented by Drinkwater and Sondergeld (2004), "People are becoming less protected over time from mortality risk, as evidenced by the decline in traditional pension plan coverage" (p. 1).

Whether DC plans—even with generous matches and investment returns—can ever provide the same benefits as DB pensions is debatable, as is whether the private annuity market can replace DB pensions. Feldstein and Ranguelova (2001) claimed that DC plans can provide the same expected benefits as DB plans. Their analysis indicates that

> the risk that future retirees would receive less in a pure defined-contribution system, than this benchmark level of benefits, would be relatively small at savings rates that would be substantially less than the future paygo [that is, pay-as-you-go] tax rate that would be required to fund that benchmark level of benefits. (p. 1116)

In other words, life annuities could be used to replicate the benefits of a DB pension. For me, writing from the perspective of the year 2012, I wonder whether the authors contemplated the dismal performance of the stock market during the last decade and the current abnormally low level of interest rates.

For those who are interested in light and accessible but comprehensive material on the U.S. market for life annuities, I recommend the Vanguard article by Zahm and Ameriks (2011) or the report by Sass, Munnell, and Eschtruth

(2011). For those interested in more general aspects of aging and financial planning, see Weierich, Kensinger, Munnell, Sass, Dickerson, Wright, and Barrett (2011). As far as the specifics of annuities are concerned, the books by Pechter (2008) for individuals and by Olsen and Kitces (2009) for financial advisers are two excellent references. Finally, for the most recent scholarly research, including a number of papers by the authors reviewed here, see Mitchell, Piggott, and Takayama (2011) or the recently published book by Warshawsky (2012), in which a number of his research articles on life annuities are collected.

4. Conclusions and Final Thoughts

To conclude my review of the vast and growing subject of life annuities, I want to point out a number of implications for practicing financial analysts that are worth emphasizing. I will then turn to imagining the future for life annuity products.

Final Takeaways of the Discussions

1. A life annuity can be viewed—and properly thought of—as a fixed-income bond that pays monthly coupons without a fixed maturity value or date. To the buyer, it looks like a portfolio of zero-coupon bonds structured to provide constant payments as long the annuitant is still alive. The periodic payments may be level, increasing at a predetermined rate, or inflation indexed. Most importantly, the yield spread above the risk-free rate is generated by the mortality credits embedded in the risk pooling. Therefore, to replicate this enhanced yield by using conventional traded instruments (e.g., regular bonds) is virtually impossible. Moreover, for people at older ages, the implied longevity yield is almost impossible to beat.

2. In general, the word "annuity" is a catchall term that does not really mean anything until it is qualified with a proper label. Financial economists, securities lawyers, insurance executives, and members of the media often talk across each other and miss each other's points because they are referring to different products. For example, there are equity-indexed annuities, tax-deferred annuities, variable annuities (with and without guaranteed living benefits), fixed annuities, deferred annuities, and, of course, fixed and variable immediate annuities. They all have the word "annuity" in their titles, but few offer the *raison d'être* of annuitization—that is, mortality credits.

3. Therefore, financial analysts and wealth managers must ensure that they understand which kind of annuity they are actually looking at before they decide to dismiss it or include it as part of a client's retirement portfolio. Even the best low-cost variable and fixed immediate annuities (i.e., those that offer pure mortality credits) can be watered down if (1) guarantees, (2) period certain (PC), or (3) refund options are added on, which are unnecessary but often added to make the annuity product palatable to the loss-averse retiree.

©2013 The Research Foundation of CFA Institute

4. A useful way to think of the benefits of a life annuity is as follows: Imagine that you and a retired neighbor both invest $500 in a money market account, with the macabre proviso that the account can be cashed-in only when one of you dies. The survivor gets the entire $1,000 plus any interest accrued, while the family of the deceased inherits nothing. (You will recognize that this arrangement is a tontine.) Now, assuming you are the survivor, your terminal investment return on the $500—whatever and whenever that might be—will far exceed the investment return from conventional stocks or bonds during that period, even though the actual money was invested in cash. Of course, the key to the supercharged return from cash is that you have to *survive* to claim the mortality credits and assets of your neighbor. For the millions of Baby Boomers retiring on a meager pension and a depleted nest egg, however, this longevity-contingent claim is likely to be the best hedge for their longevity risk. It is asset/liability management on the personal balance sheet.

5. *Longevity-risk* aversion is distinct from *financial-risk* aversion. Longevity-risk aversion is about the fear of living longer than expected and having to reduce your standard of living in retirement as a result. Individuals who are longevity-risk averse will probably consume less of their wealth early in retirement and allocate more of their nest egg to annuity products to protect against this risk. This characteristic is akin to savers who are financial-risk averse allocating more of their wealth to safer assets, such as bonds. Conceivably, those individuals who are financial-risk averse are also likely to be longevity-risk averse. In other words, counseling a retiree to buy more stocks because the person could live to be a centenarian might be internally inconsistent, at best, and an oxymoron at worst. Those who fear living a long time should own annuities. Period.

6. Most financial, public, and insurance economists would agree (something that is rare) that life annuities, longevity insurance, and guaranteed pensions have an important role to play in the optimal retirement portfolio. Noted economists—such as Brown, Mitchell, Poterba, and Warshawsky (2001)—whose works have been described in this book are only a few of those who have written extensively on the importance and role of these products in financing retirement. The debate in the literature tends to be around (1) the *optimal age*, (2) the *optimal amount*, and (3) the *optimal type* of product. Notwithstanding, all of these researchers agree that life annuities are a legitimate and core product for the optimal retirement portfolio.

7. The fact that life annuities are priced in a competitive market to account for healthier, longer-lived individuals implies that an adverse selection cost is built into these insurance products. It is not a mark-up or loading, per se, but a reflection of the clientele who are interested in acquiring life annuities. Nevertheless, buying annuities as part of a group—or perhaps making annuities mandatory for a portion of an individual's retirement account—would reduce the cost to everyone. If you can buy any insurance product in wholesale bulk as opposed to individual retail, you will save for two reasons. First, some fixed costs will be reduced, and second, and more importantly, the adverse selection costs are reduced.

8. Naturally, some individuals do not need any additional life annuities because they are already sufficiently annuitized or overannuitized. For example, anyone with a DB pension plan from an employer already has a substantial portion of wealth preannuitized. If we add to this annuity social security benefits—which can add up to a $30,000 real, or inflation-adjusted, annuity per individual—clearly many retirees do not need any more life annuity income. Moreover, if they have strong bequest motives, their optimal (additional) allocations to longevity-contingent claims should be close to zero. For wealthy, high-net-worth individuals for whom social security provides only a tiny fraction of their cash flow needs in retirement but who are not so wealthy that they can afford the legacy and bequest motives they assert, life annuities are an important class of products for them to consider.

9. Those who delay claiming U.S. Social Security (or Canadian Pension Plan) income to the latest age possible are effectively buying a real (inflation-adjusted) advanced-life delayed annuity, with a survivor benefit for the spouse. The implied longevity yield from such a strategy far exceeds the rate of return available from real or nominal bonds in today's environment of ultra-low interest rates, especially for people in better-than-average health. For them, delaying annuitization is optimal.

10. There is nothing unique or special about fixed immediate life annuities. The best way to think of life annuities is as a mortality credit overlay to a conventional asset allocation. And although most life annuities are currently bond backed (and are thus effectively a fixed-income product with some additional mortality credits), the underlying assets could be stocks, cash, or even alternative assets. Variable immediate annuities (VIAs), which are even more rarely purchased than fixed immediate annuities, are an example. **Figure 5** provides a graphical illustration of this overlay concept.

Figure 5. The Overlay Concept: Any Asset Class Can Be Annuitized

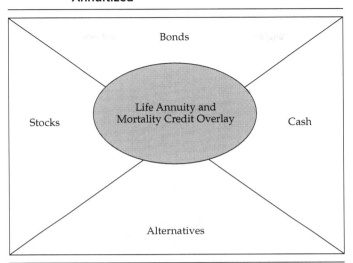

11. In the past decade or so, a number of substitutes for—and competitors with—life annuities have emerged in the form of guaranteed living benefits attached to variable annuities. The early versions of these products (2002–2006) were grossly underpriced and extremely generous, according to most researchers who carefully examined the pricing. Thus, despite the common perception that annuities were exorbitant, the embedded (put) options were not priced high enough, especially for those who knew how to optimize the value of these guarantees. Numerous insurance companies came close to the precipice as a result of offering these guarantees. Thus, in recent years, rationalization has occurred in pricing and features. Many companies, given the extreme difficulty in hedging the embedded options, most of which have maturities of 30 years or more, have withdrawn from this market altogether.

12. Behavioral evidence is growing that retirees (and seniors) who are receiving life annuity income are happier and more content with their financial condition in retirement than those receiving equivalent levels of income from other (fully liquid) sources, such as dividends, interest, and systematic withdrawal plans. Indeed, with growing concerns about dementia and Alzheimer's disease in an aging population, automatizing the retiree's income stream at the highest possible level—which is partly what a pension life annuity is all about—will become exceedingly important and valuable.

13. Credit risk, illiquidity, and low interest rates are three concerns that often are expressed by potential annuitants. Yet, all three concerns do not quite add up to an excuse for complete nonannuitization. The credit

risk is mitigated by state guarantee funds. Annuitizing only a portion of your portfolio, for example, can solve the concern regarding liquidity and access to cash in the event of a medical emergency. In addition, fears about interest rates (what if they move up suddenly tomorrow?) apply to any fixed-income instrument, not only annuities. Conservatively investing in medium-term and long-term bonds while waiting for annuity rates to increase might seem like the punch line of a joke for financial economists, but this strategy is currently being implemented by many retirees.

14. As North American Baby Boomers march toward the random ends of their life cycles, this relatively small market is likely to grow at much higher rates than it has in the past. The questions are, (1) What will life annuities look like in the future (2) and how will the features be framed to make life annuities more appealing than today?

Imagining the Life Annuity of 2020

Perhaps the next step in the evolution of retirement annuities will be a return to the past. Maybe the annuity of the year 2020 will pay out no cash at all but, instead, offer an actual *retirement service*. Allow me to explain.

One of the lesser-known facts about retirement annuities is that, despite their illustrious 2,500-year history, only in the past few hundred years have their benefits been paid in cash. For the first few thousand years, retirement annuities provided something more reliable and useful than nominal cash or coin: They paid out in units of service. For example, as I mentioned, one of the first known retirement annuities was documented in the Bible in 2 Kings 25:27–38:

> And it came to pass that the King of Babylon did lift up the head of the King of Judah out of prison . . . And he spoke kindly to him, and he did eat bread continually before him all the days of his life. And his allowance was a daily rate for every day, all the days of his life.

Thus, according to most insurance historians, one of the first retirement annuities ever was paid out in units of dinner.

During the Middle Ages, wealthy landowners and merchants purchased *corrodes* from monasteries and abbeys, which provided them with food, clothing, and often shelter for the rest of their lives. They had wealth; what they wanted was services.

The English poet and author Geoffrey Chaucer (1343–1400), at the young age of 35, so enthralled King Edward III that the king granted him a unique annuity—one gallon of wine daily for the rest of his life, to be served in the port of London. (That would be 16 glasses of wine per day, which gives me new respect for the fact that *Canterbury Tales* got written at all.)

Only in the 16th century did it become commonplace for retirement annuities to be paid and received exclusively in cash. Until then, you purchased the retirement annuity with cash but the benefit itself was denominated in units of consumption—immune to inflation and the risk of a debased currency. Perhaps the time has come to consider offering such annuities again.

Consider the following: A few years ago, the U.S. Postal Service (USPS)—an institution that itself might not be around in 2020—started offering "Forever Stamps." Although the cost of mailing a first-class letter in the United States is currently 46 cents and the price has been steadily increasing by approximately 1 cent per year, a Forever Stamp comes with no fixed monetary value. The stamp—effectively a financial derivative—entitles the holder to one unit of service, in perpetuity. The holder can use the stamp to mail one first-class (38-gram) letter anywhere in the United States forever. Pay the 46 cents today and, regardless of what it will cost to mail a first-class letter next year or 10 years hence, the cost of the service is locked in.

For the USPS, this offer is not as big a gamble as you might expect. First, by not having to print new and costly stamps every time the price goes up, the USPS saves in printing costs for the millions of people who need one- and two-cent stamps to make up the difference. At the same time, the USPS gets to keep clients' money—money it needs—while clients keep the stamps in their drawers for the next decade. All parties are winners, which is critical for true financial innovation to flourish. Other countries—Canada, New Zealand, and Singapore—offer similar stamps.

Now, think of a retirement annuity for which the benefit is modeled on a "forever" service. It might cover your water, gas, or electric bill for life. Maybe it would be denominated in units of days in a five-star nursing home or units of Lipitor, Fosamax, and Plavix. Or perhaps it is a glass of wine a day (a Chaucer mini-annuity).

The bottom line is that money is merely a medium of exchange. Even if you manage to find an entity that will guarantee you an income of $1,000 or $10,000 per month for the rest of your life—and you actually trust that the entity will be around for the rest of your life—you still run the risk that those dollars will not be enough to purchase the services you really want. In the language of finance, you are not only incurring credit risk and inflation risk, you are taking on *basis risk*—that is, a mismatch between the retirement assets you own and the liabilities that you face.

In today's interest rate environment, perhaps the hunt for yield should be abandoned in favor of the hunt for institutions that can guarantee the services an aging population will need to sustain itself. Would you buy a retirement service annuity from a utility company? How about from a pharmaceutical company? An oil and gas company? Do you trust them—or like them—any less than your local insurance company?

Sure, these companies would have to contend with a host of regulatory issues if they suddenly jumped into competition with century-old insurance companies and pension funds. But I believe it is high time for someone to be disruptively innovative in the retirement income space.

How about another glass of Merlot while we wait?

BIBLIOGRAPHY

Agnew, Julie R., Lisa R. Anderson, Jeffrey R. Gerlach, and Lisa R. Szykman. 2008. "Who Chooses Annuities? An Experimental Investigation of the Role of Gender, Framing, and Defaults." *American Economic Review*, vol. 98, no. 2 (May):418–422.

Albrecht, Peter, and Raimond Maurer. 2002. "Self-Annuitization, Consumption Shortfall in Retirement and Asset Allocation: The Annuity Benchmark." *Journal of Pension Economics and Finance*, vol. 1, no. 3 (November):269–288.

Ameriks, John, Andrew Caplin, Steven Laufer, and Stijn Van Nieuwerburgh. 2011. "The Joy of Giving or Assisted Living? Using Strategic Surveys to Separate Public Care Aversion from Bequest Motives." *Journal of Finance*, vol. 66, no. 2 (April):519–561.

Avanzi, Benjamin. 2010. "What Is It That Makes the Swiss Annuitise? A Description of the Swiss Retirement System." *Australian Actuarial Journal*, vol. 16, no. 2:135–162.

Babbel, David F. 2008. "Lifetime Income for Women: A Financial Economist's Perspective." Policy Brief, Personal Finance, Wharton Financial Institutions Center.

Babbel, David F., and Craig B. Merrill. 2007a. "Investing Your Lump Sum at Retirement." Policy Brief, Personal Finance, Wharton Financial Institutions Center.

———. 2007b. "Rational Decumulation." Working Paper No. 06-14, Wharton Financial Institutions Center.

Babbel, David F., and Ravi Reddy. 2009. "Measuring the Tax Benefit of a Tax-Deferred Annuity." *Journal of Financial Planning*, vol. 22, no. 10 (October):68–83.

Ballotta, Laura, and Steven Haberman. 2003. "Valuation of Guaranteed Annuity Conversion Options." *Insurance: Mathematics and Economics*, vol. 33, no. 1 (August):87–108.

Barro, Robert J., and James W. Friedman. 1977. "On Uncertain Lifetimes." *Journal of Political Economy*, vol. 85, no. 4 (August):843–849.

Beekman, John A., and Clinton P. Fuelling. 1990. "Interest and Mortality Randomness in Some Annuities." *Insurance: Mathematics and Economics*, vol. 9, no. 2–3 (September):185–196.

Bellhouse, D.R. 2011. *Abraham De Moivre: Setting the Stage for Classical Probability and Its Applications*. Boca Raton, FL: CRC Press.

Benartzi, Shlomo, Alessandro Previtero, and Richard H. Thaler. 2011. "Annuitization Puzzles." *Journal of Economic Perspectives*, vol. 25, no. 4 (Fall):143–164.

Bernheim, B. Douglas. 1984. "Life Cycle Annuity Valuation." NBER Working Paper No. 1511 (December).

————. 1991. "How Strong Are Bequest Motives? Evidence Based on Estimates of the Demand for Life Insurance and Annuities." *Journal of Political Economy*, vol. 99, no. 5 (October):899–927.

Beshears, John, James J. Choi, David Laibson, Brigitte C. Madrian, and Stephen P. Zeldes. 2012. "What Makes Annuitization More Appealing?" NBER Working Paper No. 18575 (November).

Biggs, John H. 1969. "Alternatives in Variable Annuity Benefit Designs." *Transactions of Society of Actuaries, Part 1*, vol. 21, no. 61:495–517.

Blake, David. 1999. "Annuity Markets: Problems and Solutions." *Geneva Papers on Risk and Insurance*, vol. 24, no. 3:358–375.

Blake, David, Andrew J.G. Cairns, and Kevin Dowd. 2003. "Pensionmetrics 2: Stochastic Pension Plan Design during the Distribution Phase." *Insurance: Mathematics and Economics*, vol. 33, no. 1 (August):29–47.

Bodie, Zvi. 1990. "Pensions as Retirement Income Insurance." *Journal of Economic Literature*, vol. 28, no. 1 (March):28–49.

Bommier, Antoine, and François Le Grand. 2012. "Too Risk Averse to Purchase Insurance? A Theoretical Glance at the Annuity Puzzle." SSRN Working Paper Series No. 1991085 (16 July).

Boyle, Phelim, and Mary Hardy. 2003. "Guaranteed Annuity Options." *ASTIN Bulletin*, vol. 33, no. 2 (November):125–152.

Bravo, Jorge M., Pedro C. Real, and Carlos P. da Silva. 2009. "Participating Life Annuities Incorporating Longevity Risk Sharing Arrangements." Working paper.

Broverman, Samuel. 1986. "The Rate of Return on Life Insurance and Annuities." *Journal of Risk and Insurance*, vol. 53, no. 3 (September):419–434.

Brown, Jeffrey R. 2001. "Private Pensions, Mortality Risk and the Decision to Annuitize." *Journal of Public Economics*, vol. 82, no. 1 (October):29–62.

————. 2002. "Differential Mortality and the Value of Individual Account Retirement Annuities." In *The Distributional Aspects of Social Security and Social Security Reform*. Edited by Martin Feldstein and Jeffrey B. Liebman. Chicago: University of Chicago Press.

————. 2009. "Understanding the Role of Annuities in Retirement Planning." In *Overcoming the Saving Slump: How to Increase the Effectiveness of Financial Education and Saving Programs*. 1st ed. Edited by Annamaria Lusardi. Chicago: University of Chicago Press.

Brown, Jeffrey R., and Theo Nijman. 2011. "Opportunities for Improving Pension Wealth Decumulation in the Netherlands." Netspar Discussion Paper No. 01/2011-008 (9 March).

Brown, Jeffrey R., and James M. Poterba. 2000. "Joint Life Annuities and Annuity Demand by Married Couples." *Journal of Risk and Insurance*, vol. 67, no. 4 (December):527–553.

———. 2006. "Household Ownership of Variable Annuities." In *Tax Policy and the Economy*. Edited by James M. Poterba. Cambridge, MA: MIT Press.

Brown, Jeffrey R., Olivia S. Mitchell, and James M. Poterba. 2001. "The Role of Real Annuities and Indexed Bonds in an Individual Accounts Retirement Program." In *Risk Aspects of Investment-Based Social Security Reform*. Edited by John Y. Campbell and Martin Feldstein. Chicago: University of Chicago Press.

———. 2002. "Mortality Risk, Inflation Risk, and Annuity Products." In *Innovations in Retirement Financing*. Edited by Olivia S. Mitchell, Zvi Bodie, P. Brett Hammond, and Stephen Zeldes. Philadelphia: University of Pennsylvania Press.

Brown, Jeffrey R., Jeffrey R. Kling, Sendhil Mullainathan, and Marian V. Wrobel. 2008. "Why Don't People Insure Late-Life Consumption? A Framing Explanation of the Under-Annuitization Puzzle." *American Economic Review*, vol. 98, no. 2 (May):304–309.

Brown, Jeffrey R., Olivia S. Mitchell, James M. Poterba, and Mark J. Warshawsky. 1999. "Taxing Retirement Income: Nonqualified Annuities and Distributions from Qualified Accounts." *National Tax Journal*, vol. 53, no. 3 (September):563–591.

———. 2001. *The Role of Annuity Markets in Financing Retirement*. Cambridge, MA: MIT Press.

Brugiavini, Agar. 1993. "Uncertainty Resolution and the Timing of Annuity Purchases." *Journal of Public Economics*, vol. 50, no. 1 (January):31–62.

Brunner, Johann K., and Susanne Pech. 2008. "Optimum Taxation of Life Annuities." *Social Choice and Welfare*, vol. 30, no. 2 (February):285–303.

Buser, Stephen A., and Michael L. Smith. 1983. "Life Insurance in a Portfolio Context." *Insurance: Mathematics and Economics*, vol. 2, no. 3 (July):147–157.

Bütler, Monika, and Stefan Staubli. 2011. "Payouts in Switzerland: Explaining Developments in Annuitization." In *Securing Lifelong Retirement Income: Global Annuity Markets and Policy*. Edited by Olivia S. Mitchell, John Piggott, and Noriyuki Takayama. London: Oxford University Press.

Bütler, Monika, and Federica Teppa. 2007. "The Choice between an Annuity and a Lump Sum: Results from Swiss Pension Funds." *Journal of Public Economics*, vol. 91, no. 10 (November):1944–1966.

Bütler, Monika, Kim Peijnenburg, and Stefan Staubli. 2011. "How Much Do Means-Tested Benefits Reduce the Demand for Annuities?" CESifo Working Paper Series No. 3493 (28 June).

Bütler, Monika, Stefan Staubli, and Maria G. Zito. Forthcoming. "How Much Does Annuity Demand React to a Large Price Change?" *Scandinavian Journal of Economics*.

Cairns, Andrew J.G., David Blake, and Kevin Dowd. 2006. "Stochastic Lifestyling: Optimal Dynamic Asset Allocation for Defined Contribution Pension Plans." *Journal of Economic Dynamics & Control*, vol. 30, no. 5 (May):843–877.

———. 2008. "Modelling and Management of Mortality Risk: A Review." *Scandinavian Actuarial Journal*, vol. 2008, nos. 2–3:79–113.

Campbell, John Y., João F. Cocco, Francisco J. Gomes, and Pascal J. Maenhout. 2001. "Investing Retirement Wealth: A Life-Cycle Model." In *Risk Aspects of Investment-Based Social Security Reform*. Edited by John Y. Campbell and Martin Feldstein. Chicago: University of Chicago Press.

Cannon, Edmund, and Ian Tonks. 2005. "Survey of Annuity Pricing." Research Report No. 318, Department for Work and Pensions, Leeds, U.K.

———. 2008. *Annuity Markets*. New York City: Oxford University Press.

———. 2009. "Money's Worth of Pension Annuities." Research Report No. 563, Department for Work and Pensions, Leeds, U.K.

Cappelletti, Giuseppe, Giovanni Guazzarotti, and Pietro Tommasino. 2011. "What Determines Annuity Demand at Retirement?" Bank of Italy Economic Working Paper No. 805 (April).

Carlson, Severin, and Blair Lord. 1986. "Unisex Retirement Benefits and the Market for Annuity 'Lemons.'" *Journal of Risk and Insurance*, vol. 53, no. 3 (September):409–418.

Carriere, Jacques F. 1999. "No-Arbitrage Pricing for Life Insurance and Annuities." *Economics Letters*, vol. 64, no. 3 (September):339–342.

Carson, James M., James S. Doran, and Randy E. Dumm. 2011. "Market Discipline in the Individual Annuity Market." *Risk Management and Insurance Review*, vol. 14, no. 1 (Spring):27–47.

Chalmers, John, and Jonathan Reuter. 2012. "How Do Retirees Value Life Annuities? Evidence from Public Employees." *Review of Financial Studies*, vol. 25, no. 8 (August):2601–2634.

Charupat, Narat, and Moshe A. Milevsky. 2001. "Mortality Swaps and Tax Arbitrage in the Canadian Insurance and Annuity Markets." *Journal of Risk and Insurance*, vol. 68, no. 2 (June):277–302.

———. 2002. "Optimal Asset Allocation in Life Annuities: A Note." *Insurance: Mathematics and Economics*, vol. 30, no. 2 (April):199–209.

Charupat, Narat, Mark J. Kamstra, and Moshe A. Milevsky. 2012. "The Annuity Duration Puzzle." SSRN Working Paper Series No. 2021579 (14 March).

Chen, Peng, and Moshe A. Milevsky. 2003. "Merging Asset Allocation and Longevity Insurance: An Optimal Perspective on Payout Annuities." *Journal of Financial Planning*, vol. 16, no. 6 (June):52–62.

Chen, Peng, Roger G. Ibbotson, Moshe A. Milevsky, and Kevin X. Zhu. 2006. "Human Capital, Asset Allocation, and Life Insurance." *Financial Analysts Journal*, vol. 62, no. 1 (January/February):97–109.

Chen, Zhuliang, Ken Vetzal, and Peter A. Forsyth. 2008. "The Effect of Modelling Parameters on the Value of GMWB Guarantees." *Insurance: Mathematics and Economics*, vol. 43, no. 1 (August):165–173.

Cocco, João F., Francisco J. Gomes, and Pascal J. Maenhout. 2005. "Consumption and Portfolio Choice over the Life Cycle." *Review of Financial Studies*, vol. 18, no. 2 (Summer):491–533.

Council of Economic Advisers. 2012. "Supporting Retirement for American Families." Executive Office of the President.

Cox, Samuel H., and Yijia Lin. 2007. "Natural Hedging of Life and Annuity Mortality Risks." *North American Actuarial Journal*, vol. 11, no. 3:1–15.

Creighton, Adam, Henry Hongbo Jin, John Piggott, and Emiliano A. Valdez. 2005. "Longevity Insurance: A Missing Market." *Singapore Economic Review*, vol. 50:417–435.

Dai, Min, Yue K. Kwok, and Jianping Zong. 2008. "Guaranteed Minimum Withdrawal Benefit in Variable Annuities." *Mathematical Finance*, vol. 18, no. 4 (October):595–611.

Davidoff, Thomas. 2009. "Housing, Health, and Annuities." *Journal of Risk and Insurance*, vol. 76, no. 1 (March):31–52.

Davidoff, Thomas, Jeffrey R. Brown, and Peter A. Diamond. 2005. "Annuities and Individual Welfare." *American Economic Review*, vol. 95, no. 5 (December):1573–1590.

Davies, James B. 1981. "Uncertain Lifetime, Consumption, and Dissaving in Retirement." *Journal of Political Economy*, vol. 89, no. 3 (June):561–577.

Dellinger, Jeffrey K. 2011. "When to Commence Income Annuities." Retirement Income Solutions Enterprise.

Devolder, Pierre, and Donatien Hainaut. 2006. "The Annuity Puzzle Revisited: A Deterministic Version with Lagrangian Methods." *Belgian Actuarial Bulletin*, vol. 6, no. 1:40–48.

Di Giacinto, Marina, and Elena Vigna. 2012. "On the Sub-Optimality Cost of Immediate Annuitization in DC Pension Funds." *Central European Journal of Operations Research*, vol. 20, no. 3 (September):497–537.

Dickson, David C.M., Mary R. Hardy, and Howard R. Waters. 2009. *Actuarial Mathematics for Life Contingent Risks*. Cambridge, U.K.: Cambridge University Press.

Direr, Alexis. 2010. "Flexible Life Annuities." *Journal of Public Economic Theory*, vol. 12, no. 1 (February):43–55.

Dowd, Kevin, David Blake, and Andrew J.G. Cairns. 2011. "A Computationally Efficient Algorithm for Estimating the Distribution of Future Annuity Values under Interest-Rate and Longevity Risks." *North American Actuarial Journal*, vol. 15, no. 2:237–247.

Drinkwater, Matthew, and Eric T. Sondergeld. 2004. "Perceptions of Mortality Risk: Implications for Annuities." In *Pension Design and Structure: New Lessons from Behavioral Finance*. Edited by Olivia S. Mitchell and Stephen P. Utkus. New York City: Oxford University Press.

Duncan, Robert M. 1952. "A Retirement System Granting Unit Annuities and Investing in Equities." *Transactions of Society of Actuaries*, vol. 4, no. 10:317–344.

Dushi, Irena, and Anthony Webb. 2004. "Household Annuitization Decisions: Simulations and Empirical Analyses." *Journal of Pension Economics and Finance*, vol. 3, no. 2 (July):109–143.

Eckstein, Zvi, Martin Eichenbaum, and Dan Peled. 1985a. "Uncertain Lifetimes and the Welfare Enhancing Properties of Annuity Markets and Social Security." *Journal of Public Economics*, vol. 26, no. 3 (April):303–326.

———. 1985b. "The Distribution of Wealth and Welfare in the Presence of Incomplete Annuity Markets." *Quarterly Journal of Economics*, vol. 100, no. 3 (August):789–806.

Edwards, Ryan D. 2012. "The Cost of Uncertain Life Span." *Journal of Population Economics* (February).

Fehr, Hans, and Christian Habermann. 2008. "Welfare Effects of Life Annuities: Some Clarifications." *Economics Letters*, vol. 99, no. 1 (April):177–180.

Feigenbaum, James, and Emin Gahramanov. 2012. "Is It Really Good to Annuitize?" Working paper, Economic Series No. 2012 (1), Deakin University, Faculty of Business and Law, School of Accounting, Economics and Finance (6 March).

Feldstein, Martin, and Elena Ranguelova. 2001. "Individual Risk in an Investment-Based Social Security System." *American Economic Review*, vol. 91, no. 4 (September):1116–1125.

Finkelstein, Amy, and James Poterba. 2002. "Selection Effects in the United Kingdom Individual Annuities Market." *Economic Journal*, vol. 112, no. 476 (January):28–50.

———. 2004. "Adverse Selection in Insurance Markets: Policyholder Evidence from the U.K. Annuity Market." *Journal of Political Economy*, vol. 112, no. 1 (February):183–208.

Finkelstein, Amy, James Poterba, and Casey Rothschild. 2009. "Redistribution by Insurance Market Regulation: Analyzing a Ban on Gender-Based Retirement Annuities." *Journal of Financial Economics*, vol. 91, no. 1 (January):38–58.

Fischer, Stanley. 1973. "A Life Cycle Model of Life Insurance Purchases." *International Economic Review*, vol. 14, no. 1 (February):132–152.

Fisher, Irving. 1930. *The Theory of Interest: As Determined by Impatience to Spend Income and Opportunity to Invest It*. New York City: Macmillan.

Fong, Joelle H.Y., Jean Lemaire, and Yiu K. Tse. 2011. "Improving Money's Worth Ratio Calculations: The Case of Singapore's Pension Annuities." SSRN Working Paper Series No. 1928323 (7 September).

Fong, Joelle H.Y., Olivia S. Mitchell, and Benedict S.K. Koh. 2011. "Longevity Risk Management in Singapore's National Pension System." *Journal of Risk and Insurance*, vol. 78, no. 4 (December):961–982.

Fornero, Elsa, and Elisa Luciano, eds. 2004. *Developing an Annuity Market in Europe*. Northampton, MA: Edward Elgar Publishing.

Freedman, Barry. 2008. "Efficient Post-Retirement Asset Allocation." *North American Actuarial Journal*, vol. 12, no. 3:228–241.

Frees, Edward W., Jacques Carriere, and Emiliano Valdez. 1996. "Annuity Valuation with Dependent Mortality." *Journal of Risk and Insurance*, vol. 63, no. 2 (June):229–261.

Friedman, Benjamin M., and Mark J. Warshawsky. 1990. "The Cost of Annuities: Implications for Saving Behaviour and Bequests." *Quarterly Journal of Economics*, vol. 105, no. 1:135–154.

Friedman, Milton. 1957. *A Theory of the Consumption Function*. Princeton, NJ: Princeton University Press.

Gale, William G., J.M. Iwry, David C. John, and Lina Walker. 2008. "Increasing Annuitization in 401(k) Plans with Automatic Trial Income." The Retirement Security Project, Brookings Institution.

Ganegoda, Amandha, and Hazel Bateman. 2008. "Australia's Disappearing Market for Life Annuities." Centre for Pensions and Superannuation Discussion Paper 2008-1.

Gazzale, Robert S., and Lina Walker. 2009. "Behavioral Biases in Annuity Choice: An Experiment." Williams College Economics Department Working Paper Series No. 2009-01.

Gerrard, Russell, Steven Haberman, and Elena Vigna. 2004. "Optimal Investment Choices Post-Retirement in a Defined Contribution Pension Scheme." *Insurance: Mathematics and Economics*, vol. 35, no. 2 (October):321–342.

Goda, Gopi S., and Colin M. Ramsay. 2007. "Determining the Optimum Guarantee Period for a One-Life Retirement Annuity." *North American Actuarial Journal*, vol. 11, no. 3:100–112.

Goldsticker, Ralph. 2007. "A Mutual Fund to Yield Annuity-Like Benefits." *Financial Analysts Journal*, vol. 63, no. 1 (January/February):63–67.

Gong, Guan, and Anthony Webb. 2008. "Mortality Heterogeneity and the Distributional Consequences of Mandatory Annuitization." *Journal of Risk and Insurance*, vol. 75, no. 4 (December):1055–1079.

———. 2010. "Evaluating the Advanced Life Deferred Annuity—An Annuity People Might Actually Buy." *Insurance: Mathematics and Economics*, vol. 46, no. 1 (February):210–221.

Goodman, Benjamin, and Michael Heller. 2006. "Annuities: Now, Later, Never?" *TIAA-CREF Institute Trends and Issues*.

Gunawardena, Dmitri, Christopher Hicks, and David O'Neill. 2008. "Pension Annuities: Pension Annuities and the Open Market Solution." Research Paper No. 8, Research Department, Association of British Insurers.

Gupta, Aparna, and Zhisheng Li. 2007. "Integrating Optimal Annuity Planning with Consumption–Investment Selections in Retirement Planning." *Insurance: Mathematics and Economics*, vol. 41, no. 1 (July):96–110.

Hainaut, Donatien, and Pierre Devolder. 2006. "Life Annuitization: Why and How Much?" *ASTIN Bulletin*, vol. 36, no. 2:629–654.

Hakansson, Nils H. 1969. "Optimal Investment and Consumption Strategies under Risk, an Uncertain Lifetime, and Insurance." *International Economic Review*, vol. 10, no. 3 (October):443–466.

Halley, Edmond. 1693. "An Estimate of the Degrees of the Mortality of Mankind, Drawn from the Curious Tables of the Births and Funerals at the City of Breslaw." *Philosophical Transactions*, vol. 17:596–610.

Hamermesh, Daniel S. 1985. "Expectations, Life Expectancy, and Economic Behavior." *Quarterly Journal of Economics*, vol. 100, no. 2 (May):389–408.

Hansen, Gary D., and Selahattin İmrohoroğlu. 2008. "Consumption over the Life Cycle: The Role of Annuities." *Review of Economic Dynamics*, vol. 11, no. 3 (July):566–583.

Horneff, Wolfram J., Raimond Maurer, and Ralph Rogalla. 2010. "Dynamic Portfolio Choice with Deferred Annuities." *Journal of Banking & Finance*, vol. 34, no. 11 (November):2652–2664.

Horneff, Wolfram J., Raimond H. Maurer, and Michael Z. Stamos. 2008. "Life-Cycle Asset Allocation with Annuity Markets." *Journal of Economic Dynamics & Control*, vol. 32, no. 11 (November):3590–3612.

Horneff, Wolfram J., Raimond H. Maurer, Olivia S. Mitchell, and Ivica Dus. 2008. "Following the Rules: Integrating Asset Allocation and Annuitization in Retirement Portfolios." *Insurance: Mathematics and Economics*, vol. 42, no. 1 (February):396–408.

Horneff, Wolfram J., Raimond H. Maurer, Olivia S. Mitchell, and Michael Z. Stamos. 2009. "Asset Allocation and Location over the Life Cycle with Investment-Linked Survival-Contingent Payouts." *Journal of Banking & Finance*, vol. 33, no. 9 (September):1688–1699.

———. 2010. "Variable Payout Annuities and Dynamic Portfolio Choice in Retirement." *Journal of Pension Economics and Finance*, vol. 9, no. 2 (April):163–183.

Hu, Wei-Yin, and Jason S. Scott. 2007. "Behavioral Obstacles in the Annuity Market." *Financial Analysts Journal*, vol. 63, no. 6 (November/December):71–82.

Huebner, Solomon S. 1927. *The Economics of Life Insurance: Human Life Values, Their Financial Organization, Management, and Liquidation.* New York City: D. Appleton-Century Company.

Hurd, Michael D. 1989. "Mortality Risk and Bequests." *Econometrica*, vol. 57, no. 4 (July):779–813.

Hurd, Michael D., Constantijn W.A. Panis, James P. Smith, and Julie M. Zissimopoulos. 2004. "Pension Annuitization and Social Security Claiming." In *Developing an Annuity Market in Europe.* Edited by Elsa Fornero and Elisa Luciano. Northampton, MA: Edward Elgar Publishing.

Ibbotson, Roger G., Moshe A. Milevsky, Peng Chen, and Kevin X. Zhu. 2007. *Lifetime Financial Advice: Human Capital, Asset Allocation, and Insurance.* Charlottesville, VA: Research Foundation of CFA Institute.

Inkmann, Joachim, Paula Lopes, and Alexander Michaelides. 2011. "How Deep Is the Annuity Market Participation Puzzle?" *Review of Financial Studies*, vol. 24, no. 1 (January):279–319.

James, Estelle, and Renuka Sane. 2003. "The Annuity Market in India: Do Consumers Get Their Money's Worth? What Are the Key Public Policy Issues?" In *Rethinking Pension Provision for India.* Edited by Anand Bordia and Gautam Bhardwaj. Noida, India: Tata McGraw-Hill.

James, Estelle, and Xue Song. 2001. "Annuities Markets around the World: Money's Worth and Risk Intermediation." Center for Research on Pensions and Welfare Policies Working Paper No. 16/01.

James, Estelle, and Dimitri Vittas. 2001. "Annuity Markets in Comparative Perspective: Do Consumers Get Their Money's Worth?" In *OECD Private Pensions Conference 2000.* Paris: OECD.

James, Estelle, Guillermo Martinez, and Augusto Iglesias. 2006. "The Payout Stage in Chile: Who Annuitizes and Why?" *Journal of Pension Economics and Finance*, vol. 5, no. 2 (July):121–154.

Jang, Bong-Gyu, Hyeng K. Koo, and Ho-Seok Lee. 2010. "Default Risk of Life Annuity and the Annuity Puzzle." Working paper.

Jennings, Robert M., and Andrew P. Trout. 1982. *The Tontine: From the Reign of Louis XIV to the French Revolutionary Era*. S.S. Huebner Foundation for Insurance Education, Wharton School, University of Pennsylvania.

Jennings, Robert M., Donald F. Swanson, and Andrew P. Trout. 1988. "Alexander Hamilton's Tontine Proposal." *William and Mary Quarterly*, vol. 45, no. 1 (January):107–115.

Jiménez-Martín, Sergi, and Alfonso R. Sánchez Martín. 2007. "An Evaluation of the Life Cycle Effects of Minimum Pensions on Retirement Behaviour." *Journal of Applied Econometrics*, vol. 22, no. 5 (August):923–950.

Jousten, Alain. 2001. "Life-Cycle Modeling of Bequests and Their Impact on Annuity Valuation." *Journal of Public Economics*, vol. 79, no. 1 (January):149–177.

Kaplan, Paul D. 2006. "Asset Allocation with Annuities for Retirement Income Management." *Journal of Wealth Management*, vol. 8, no. 4 (Spring):27–40.

Kapur, Sandeep, and J.M. Orszag. 1999. "A Portfolio Approach to Investment and Annuitization during Retirement." Mimeo. London: Birbeck College, University of London.

Kartashov, Vasily, Raimond Maurer, Olivia S. Mitchell, and Ralph Rogalla. 2011. "Lifecycle Portfolio Choices with Systematic Longevity Risk and Variable Investments-Linked Deferred Annuities." NBER Working Paper No. 17505 (October).

Khorasanee, M.Z. 1996. "Annuity Choices for Pensioners." *Journal of Actuarial Practice*, vol. 4, no. 2:229–255.

Kingston, Geoffrey, and Susan Thorp. 2005. "Annuitization and Asset Allocation with HARA Utility." *Journal of Pension Economics and Finance*, vol. 4, no. 3 (November):225–248.

Koijen, Ralph S.J., Theo E. Nijman, and Bas J.M. Werker. 2011. "Optimal Annuity Risk Management." *Review of Finance*, vol. 15, no. 4 (October):799–833.

Kopf, E.W. 1927. "The Early History of the Annuity." *Proceedings of the Casualty Actuarial Society*, vol. 13, no. 28:225–266.

Kotlikoff, Laurence J., and Avia Spivak. 1981. "The Family as an Incomplete Annuities Market." *Journal of Political Economy*, vol. 89, no. 2 (April):372–391.

Kotlikoff, Laurence J., John Shoven, and Avia Spivak. 1986. "The Effect of Annuity Insurance on Savings and Inequality." *Journal of Labor Economics*, vol. 4, no. 3 (July):S183–S207.

Kwon, Hyuk-Sung, and Bruce L. Jones. 2006. "The Impact of Determinants of Mortality on Life Insurance and Annuities." *Insurance: Mathematics and Economics*, vol. 38, no. 2 (April):271–288.

Lachance, Marie-Eve. 2012. "Optimal Onset and Exhaustion of Retirement Savings in a Life-Cycle Model." *Journal of Pension Economics and Finance*, vol. 11, no. 1 (January):21–52.

Lewin, C.G. 2003. *Pensions and Insurance before 1800: A Social History*. East Lothian, U.K.: Tuckwell Press.

Lieber, Ron. 2010. "The Unloved Annuity Gets a Hug from Obama." *New York Times* (29 January): www.nytimes.com/2010/01/30/your-money/annuities/30money.html.

LIMRA. 2010. "U.S. Individual Annuity Yearbook." Windsor, CT.

Lin, Yijia, and Samuel H. Cox. 2005. "Securitization of Mortality Risks in Life Annuities." *Journal of Risk and Insurance*, vol. 72, no. 2 (June):227–252.

Lockwood, Lee M. 2012. "Bequest Motives and the Annuity Puzzle." *Review of Economic Dynamics*, vol. 15, no. 2 (April):226–243.

Lopes, Paula, and Alexander Michaelides. 2007. "Rare Events and Annuity Market Participation." *Finance Research Letters*, vol. 4, no. 2 (June):82–91.

Macdonald, Angus, and Kenneth McIvor. 2010. "Pensions and Genetics: Can Longevity Genes Be Reliable Risk Factors for Annuity Pricing?" *Scandinavian Actuarial Journal*, vol. 2010, no. 1:1–14.

Mackenzie, George A. 2006. *Annuity Markets and Pension Reform*. New York City: Cambridge University Press.

MacMinn, Richard, Patrick Brockett, and David Blake. 2006. "Longevity Risk and Capital Markets." *Journal of Risk and Insurance*, vol. 73, no. 4 (December):551–557.

McCarthy, David, and Olivia S. Mitchell. 2004. "Annuities for an Ageing World." In *Developing an Annuity Market in Europe*. Edited by Elsa Fornero and Elisa Luciano. Northampton, MA: Edward Elgar Publishing.

———. 2010. "International Adverse Selection in Life Insurance and Annuities." In *Ageing in Advanced Industrial States: Riding the Age Waves*, vol. 3. 1st ed. Edited by Shripad Tuljapurkar, Naohiro Ogawa, and Anne H. Gauthier. New York City: Springer.

McQueen, Rod. 1997. *Who Killed Confederation Life: The Inside Story*. Toronto: McClelland and Stewart.

Mehr, Robert I. 1958. "The Variable Annuity: Security or Insurance." *Journal of Finance*, vol. 13, no. 3 (September):386–411.

Menoncin, Francesco. 2008. "The Role of Longevity Bonds in Optimal Portfolios." *Insurance: Mathematics and Economics*, vol. 42, no. 1 (February):343–358.

Mereu, John A. 1962. "Annuity Values Directly from the Makeham Constants." *Transaction of Society of Actuaries*, vol. 14:269–286.

Merton, Robert C. 1971. "Optimum Consumption and Portfolio Rules in a Continuous-Time Model." *Journal of Economic Theory*, vol. 3, no. 4 (December):373–413.

Milevsky, Moshe A. 1998. "Optimal Asset Allocation towards the End of the Life Cycle: To Annuitize or Not to Annuitize?" *Journal of Risk and Insurance*, vol. 65, no. 3 (September):401–426.

———. 2005a. "Real Longevity Insurance with a Deductible: Introduction to Advanced-Life Delayed Annuities (ALDA)." *North American Actuarial Journal*, vol. 9, no. 4:109–122.

———. 2005b. "The Implied Longevity Yield: A Note on Developing an Index for Life Annuities." *Journal of Risk and Insurance*, vol. 72, no. 2 (June):302–320.

———. 2006. *The Calculus of Retirement Income: Financial Models for Pension and Insurance*. New York City: Cambridge University Press.

———. 2011. "Spending Retirement on Planet Vulcan: The Impact of Longevity Risk Aversion on Optimal Withdrawal Rates." *Financial Analysts Journal*, vol. 67, no. 2 (March/April):45–58.

———. 2012. *The Seven Most Important Equations for Your Retirement*. Toronto: John Wiley & Sons Canada.

———. Forthcoming 2013. *Tontines: How a Fascinating but Neglected Annuity Scheme Can Help Reduce the Cost of Retirement*.

Milevsky, Moshe A., and Huaxiong Huang. 2011. "Spending Retirement on Planet Vulcan: The Impact of Longevity Risk Aversion on Optimal Withdrawal Rates." *Financial Analysts Journal*, vol. 67, no. 2 (March/April):45–58.

Milevsky, Moshe A., and Vlad Kyrychenko. 2008. "Portfolio Choice with Puts: Evidence from Variable Annuities." *Financial Analysts Journal*, vol. 64, no. 2 (March/April):1–30.

Milevsky, Moshe A., and Steven E. Posner. 2001. "The Titanic Option: Valuation of Guaranteed Minimum Death Benefit in Variable Annuities and Mutual Funds." *Journal of Risk and Insurance*, vol. 68, no. 1 (March):93–128.

Milevsky, Moshe A., and S. David Promislow. 2001. "Mortality Derivatives and the Option to Annuitise." *Insurance: Mathematics and Economics*, vol. 29, no. 3 (December):299–318.

Milevsky, Moshe A., and Chris Robinson. 2005. "A Sustainable Spending Rate without Simulation." *Financial Analysts Journal*, vol. 61, no. 6 (November/December):89–100.

Milevsky, Moshe A., and Thomas S. Salisbury. 2006. "Financial Valuation of Guaranteed Minimum Withdrawal Benefits." *Insurance: Mathematics and Economics*, vol. 38, no. 1 (February):21–38.

Milevsky, Moshe A., and Virginia R. Young. 2007a. "Annuitization and Asset Allocation." *Journal of Economic Dynamics and Control*, vol. 31, no. 9 (September):3138–3177.

Milevsky, Moshe A., and Virginia R. Young. 2007b. "The Timing of Annuitization: Investment Dominance and Mortality Risk." *Insurance: Mathematics and Economics*, vol. 40, no. 1 (January):135–144.

Mirer, Thad W. 1979. "The Wealth–Age Relation among the Aged." *American Economic Review*, vol. 69, no. 3 (June):435–443.

Mitchell, Olivia S., and David McCarthy. 2002. "Estimating International Adverse Selection in Annuities." *North American Actuarial Journal*, vol. 6, no. 4:38–54.

Mitchell, Olivia S., John Piggott, and Noriyuki Takayama. 2011. *Securing Lifelong Retirement Income: Global Annuity Markets and Policy.* Oxford, U.K.: Oxford University Press.

Mitchell, Olivia S., James M. Poterba, Mark J. Warshawsky, and Jeffrey R. Brown. 1999. "New Evidence on the Money's Worth of Individual Annuities." *American Economic Review*, vol. 89, no. 5 (December):1299–1318.

Modigliani, Franco. 1986. "Life Cycle, Individual Thrift, and the Wealth of Nations." *American Economic Review*, vol. 76, no. 3 (June):297–313.

Mottola, Gary R., and Stephen P. Utkus. 2007. "Lump Sum or Annuity? An Analysis of Choice in DB Pension Payouts." *Vanguard Center for Retirement Research*, vol. 30:1–10.

Mudavanhu, Blessing, and Jun Zhuo. 2002. "Valuing Guaranteed Minimum Death Benefits in Variable Annuities and the Option to Lapse." Working paper, Haas School of Business, University of California, Berkeley.

Munnell, Alicia H., Francesca Golub-Sass, Mauricio Soto, and Francis Vitagliano. 2007. "Why Are Healthy Employers Freezing Their Pensions?" *Journal of Pension Benefits*, vol. 14, no. 4:3–14.

Murray, Michael L., and Stuart Klugman. 1990. "Impaired Health Life Annuities." *Journal of the American Society of CLU and ChFC*, vol. 44, no. 5:50–58.

Murtaugh, Christopher M., Brenda C. Spillman, and Mark J. Warshawsky. 2001. "In Sickness and in Health: An Annuity Approach to Financing Long-Term Care and Retirement Income." *Journal of Risk and Insurance*, vol. 68, no. 2 (June):225–253.

Nielson, Norma L. 2012. "Annuities and Your Nest Egg: Reforms to Promote Optimal Annuitization of Retirement." C.D. Howe Commentary No. 358 (16 August).

Olsen, John, and Michael E. Kitces. 2009. *The Annuity Advisor.* 2nd ed. Cincinnati: The National Underwriter Company.

Pang, Gaobo, and Mark J. Warshawsky. 2009. "Comparing Strategies for Retirement Wealth Management: Mutual Funds and Annuities." *Journal of Financial Planning*, vol. 22, no. 8 (August):36–47.

Pang, Gaobo, and Mark J. Warshawsky. 2010. "Optimizing the Equity-Bond Annuity Portfolio in Retirement: The Impact of Uncertain Health Expenses." *Insurance: Mathematics and Economics*, vol. 46, no. 1 (February):198–209.

Panis, Constantijn W.A. 2004. "Annuities and Retirement Well-Being." In *Pension Design and Structure: New Lessons from Behavioral Finance*. Edited by Olivia S. Mitchell and Stephen P. Utkus. Oxford, U.K.: Oxford University Press.

Park, Youngkyun. 2011. "Retirement Income Adequacy with Immediate and Longevity Annuities." *Employee Benefit Research Institute*, Issue Brief No. 357.

Pashchenko, Svetlana. 2010. "Accounting for Non-Annuitization." Working Paper No. 2010-03, Federal Reserve Bank of Chicago.

Pecchenino, Rowena A., and Patricia S. Pollard. 1997. "The Effects of Annuities, Bequests, and Aging in an Overlapping Generations Model of Endogenous Growth." *Economic Journal*, vol. 107, no. 440 (January):26–46.

Pechter, Kerry. 2008. *Annuities for Dummies*. Indianapolis: Wiley Publishing.

Peijnenburg, Kim, Theo Nijman, and Bas J.M. Werker. 2012. "Health Cost Risk, Incomplete Markets, or Bequest Motives—Revisiting the Annuity Puzzle." Working paper.

Philipson, Tomas J., and Gary S. Becker. 1998. "Old-Age Longevity and Mortality-Contingent Claims." *Journal of Political Economy*, vol. 106, no. 3 (June):551–573.

Piggott, John, Emiliano A. Valdez, and Bettina Detzel. 2005. "The Simple Analytics of a Pooled Annuity Fund." *Journal of Risk and Insurance*, vol. 72, no. 3 (September):497–520.

Pliska, Stanley R., and Jinchun Ye. 2007. "Optimal Life Insurance Purchase and Consumption/Investment under Uncertain Lifetime." *Journal of Banking & Finance*, vol. 31, no. 5 (May):1307–1319.

Post, Thomas, Helmut Gründl, and Hato Schmeiser. 2006. "Portfolio Management and Retirement: What Is the Best Arrangement for a Family?" *Financial Markets and Portfolio Management*, vol. 20, no. 3 (September):265–285.

Poterba, James M. 2001. "Annuity Markets and Retirement Security." *Fiscal Studies*, vol. 22, no. 3 (September):249–270.

———. 2005. "Annuities in Early Modern Europe." In *The Origins of Value: The Financial Innovations that Created Modern Capital Markets*. Edited by William N. Goetzmann and K. Geert Rouwenhorst. Oxford, U.K.: Oxford University Press.

Previtero, Alessandro. 2011. "Stock Market Returns and Annuitization: A Case of Myopic Extrapolation." SSRN Working Paper Series No. 1787123.

Promislow, S. David. 2011. *Fundamentals of Actuarial Mathematics.* 2nd ed. Chichester, U.K.: John Wiley & Sons.

Purcal, Sachi, and John Piggott. 2008. "Explaining Low Annuity Demand: An Optimal Portfolio Application to Japan." *Journal of Risk and Insurance*, vol. 75, no. 2 (June):493–516.

Ransom, Roger L., and Richard Sutch. 1987. "Tontine Insurance and the Armstrong Investigation: A Case of Stifled Innovation, 1868–1905." *Journal of Economic History*, vol. 47, no. 2 (June):379–390.

Reichenstein, William. 2003. "Allocation during Retirement: Adding Annuities to the Mix." *Journal of the American Association of Individual Investors* (November):3–9.

Richard, Scott F. 1975. "Optimal Consumption, Portfolio and Life Insurance Rules for an Uncertain Lived Individual in a Continuous Time Model." *Journal of Financial Economics*, vol. 2, no. 2 (June):187–203.

Robinson, S., and A. Fliegelman. 2002. "The U.S. Payout Annuity Market." Moody's Investors Service, Special Comment (August).

Rocha, Roberto, Dimitri Vittas, and Heinz P. Rudolph. 2011. "Annuities and Other Retirement Products: Designing the Payout Phase." International Bank for Reconstruction and Development, World Bank, Washington, DC.

Rotemberg, Julio J. 2009. "Can a Continuously-Liquidating Tontine (or Mutual Inheritance Fund) Succeed Where Immediate Annuities Have Floundered?" Working Paper 09-121, Harvard Business School.

Rothschild, Casey G. 2009. "Adverse Selection in Annuity Markets: Evidence from the British Life Annuity Act of 1808." *Journal of Public Economics*, vol. 93, no. 5–6 (June):776–784.

Salm, Martin. 2011. "The Effect of Pensions on Longevity: Evidence from Union Army Veterans." *Economic Journal*, vol. 121, no. 552 (May):595–619.

Samuelson, Paul A. 1969. "Lifetime Portfolio Selection by Dynamic Stochastic Programming." *Review of Economics and Statistics*, vol. 51, no. 3 (August):239–246.

Sass, Steven, Alicia H. Munnell, and Andrew Eschtruth. 2011. "Managing Your Money in Retirement." Financial Security Project, Boston College.

Schulze, Roman N., and Thomas Post. 2010. "Individual Annuity Demand under Aggregate Mortality Risk." *Journal of Risk and Insurance*, vol. 77, no. 2 (June):423–449.

Scott, Jason S., John G. Watson, and Wei-Yin Hu. 2011. "What Makes a Better Annuity?" *Journal of Risk and Insurance*, vol. 78, no. 1:213–244.

Sexauer, Stephen C., and Laurence B. Siegel. 2013. "A Pension Promise to Oneself." Working paper.

Sexauer, Stephen C., Michael W. Peskin, and Daniel Cassidy. 2012. "Making Retirement Income Last a Lifetime." *Financial Analysts Journal*, vol. 68, no. 1 (January/February):74–84.

Shah, Premal, and Dimitris Bertsimas. 2008. "An Analysis of the Guaranteed Withdrawal Benefits for Life Option." SSRN Working Paper Series No. 1312727.

Shankar, S.G. 2009. "A New Strategy to Guarantee Retirement Income Using TIPS and Longevity Insurance." *Financial Services Review*, vol. 18, no. 1 (Spring):53–68.

Sharpe, William F. 1964. "Capital Asset Prices: A Theory of Market Equilibrium under Conditions of Risk." *Journal of Finance*, vol. 19, no. 3 (September):425–442.

Sheshinski, Eytan. 2007. "Optimum and Risk-Class Pricing of Annuities." *Economic Journal*, vol. 117, no. 516 (January):240–251.

———. 2008. *The Economic Theory of Annuities*. Princeton, NJ: Princeton University Press.

———. 2010. "Refundable Annuities (Annuity Options)." *Journal of Public Economic Theory*, vol. 12, no. 1 (February):7–21.

Shi, Zhen. 2008. "Annuitization and Retirement Timing Decisions." SSRN Working Paper Series No. 1516834.

Sinclair, Sven H., and Kent A. Smetters. 2004. "Health Shocks and the Demand for Annuities." Congressional Budget Office Technical Paper 2004–09.

Sinha, Tapen. 1986. "The Effects of Survival Probabilities, Transactions Cost and the Attitude towards Risk on the Demand for Annuities." *Journal of Risk and Insurance*, vol. 53, no. 2 (June):301–307.

Soares, Chris, and Mark J. Warshawsky. 2004. "Annuity Risk: Volatility and Inflation Exposure in Payments from Immediate Life Annuities." In *Developing an Annuity Market in Europe*. Edited by Elsa Fornero and Elisa Luciano. Northampton, MA: Edward Elgar Publishing.

Stabile, Gabriele. 2006. "Optimal Timing of the Annuity Purchase: Combined Stochastic Control and Optimal Stopping Problem." *International Journal of Theoretical and Applied Finance*, vol. 9, no. 2 (March):151–170.

Stevens, Ralph. 2009. "Annuity Decisions with Systematic Longevity Risk." Working paper.

Sun, Wei, and Anthony Webb. 2011. "Valuing the Longevity Insurance Acquired by Delayed Claiming of Social Security." *Journal of Risk and Insurance*, vol. 78, no. 4 (December):907–930.

©2013 The Research Foundation of CFA Institute

Sundaresan, Suresh, and Fernando Zapatero. 1997. "Valuation, Optimal Asset Allocation and Retirement Incentives of Pension Plans." *Review of Financial Studies*, vol. 10, no. 3 (July):631–660.

Telford, Peter G., Bridget A. Browne, Ed J. Collinge, Paul Fulcher, Ben E. Johnson, Wendy Little, Joseph L.C. Lu, Jeremy M. Nurse, Derek W. Smith, and Feifei Zhang. 2011. "Developments in the Management of Annuity Business." *British Actuarial Journal*, vol. 16, no. 3 (September):471–551.

Teppa, Federica. 2011. "Can the Longevity Risk Alleviate the Annuitization Puzzle? Empirical Evidence from Dutch Data." Working Paper No. 302, De Nederlandsche Bank.

Tergesen, Anne, and Leslie Scism. 2009. "Getting Smart about Annuities." *Wall Street Journal* (18 April): http://online.wsj.com/article/SB123972531986417405.html.

Vidal-Meliá, Carlos, and Ana Lejárraga-García. 2006. "Demand for Life Annuities from Married Couples with a Bequest Motive." *Journal of Pension Economics and Finance*, vol. 5, no. 2 (July):197–229.

Walliser, Jan. 2000. "Adverse Selection in the Annuities Market and the Impact of Privatizing Social Security." *Scandinavian Journal of Economics*, vol. 102, no. 3 (September):373–393.

Wang, Ting, and Virginia R. Young. 2012. "Optimal Commutable Annuities to Minimize the Probability of Lifetime Ruin." *Insurance: Mathematics and Economics*, vol. 50, no. 1 (January):200–216.

Waring, M. Barton. 2004a. "Liability-Relative Investing." *Journal of Portfolio Management*, vol. 30, no. 4 (Summer):8–20.

———. 2004b. "Liability-Relative Investing II." *Journal of Portfolio Management*, vol. 31, no. 1 (Fall):40–53.

Warner, John T., and Saul Pleeter. 2001. "The Personal Discount Rate, Evidence from Military Downsizing Programs." *American Economic Review*, vol. 91, no. 1 (March):33–53.

Warshawsky, Mark J. 1988. "Private Annuity Markets in the United States: 1919–1984." *Journal of Risk and Insurance*, vol. 55, no. 3 (September):518–528.

———. 2012. *Retirement Income: Risks and Strategies*. Cambridge, MA: MIT Press.

Webb, Anthony. 2011. "The U.S. Longevity Insurance Market." In *Securing Lifelong Retirement Income: Global Annuity Markets and Policy*. Edited by Olivia S. Mitchell, John Piggott, and Noriyuki Takayama. Oxford, U.K.: Oxford University Press.

Weierich, Mariann R., Elizabeth A. Kensinger, Alicia H. Munnell, Steven A. Sass, Brad C. Dickerson, Christoper I. Wright, and Lisa F. Barrett. 2011. "Older and Wiser? An Affective Science Perspective on Age-Related Challenges in Financial Decision Making." *Social Cognitive and Affective Neuroscience*, vol. 6, no. 2 (April):195–206.

Williams, Arthur C. 1986. "Higher Interest Rates, Longer Lifetimes, and the Demand for Life Annuities." *Journal of Risk and Insurance*, vol. 53, no. 1 (March):164–171.

Yaari, Menahem E. 1964. "On the Consumer's Lifetime Allocation Process." *International Economic Review*, vol. 5, no. 3 (September):304–317.

———. 1965. "Uncertain Lifetime, Life Insurance and the Theory of the Consumer." *Review of Economic Studies*, vol. 32, no. 2 (April):137–150.

Yagi, Tadashi, and Yasuyuki Nishigaki. 1993. "The Inefficiency of Private Constant Annuities." *Journal of Risk and Insurance*, vol. 60, no. 3 (September):385–412.

Yogo, Motohiro. 2011. "Portfolio Choice in Retirement: Health Risk and the Demand for Annuities, Housing, and Risky Assets." SSRN Working Paper Series No. 1085306.

Zahm, Nathan, and John Ameriks. 2011. "Estimating Internal Rates of Return on Income Annuities." Vanguard Research.

Zeng, Lulu. 2010. "Optimal Consumption and Portfolio Choice for Retirees." SSRN Working Paper Series No. 1327989.

RESEARCH FOUNDATION CONTRIBUTION FORM

☑ **Yes**, I want the Research Foundation to continue to fund innovative research that advances the investment management profession. Please accept my tax-deductible contribution at the following level:

Thought Leadership Circle .... US$1,000,000 or more
Named Endowment .... US$100,000 to US$999,999
Research Fellow .... US$10,000 to US$99,999
Contributing Donor .... US$1,000 to US$9,999
Friend .... Up to US$999

I would like to donate $ _____.

☐ My check is enclosed (payable to the Research Foundation of CFA Institute).
☐ I would like to donate appreciated securities (send me information).
☐ Please charge my donation to my credit card.
　　■ VISA　■ MC　■ Amex　■ Diners　■ Corporate　■ Personal

| | | | | | | | | | | | | | | | |
|—|—|—|—|—|—|—|—|—|—|—|—|—|—|—|—|

Card Number

___/___
Expiration Date

_____
Name on card　PLEASE PRINT

☐ Corporate Card
☐ Personal Card

_____
Signature

☐ This is a pledge. Please bill me for my donation of $ _____
☐ I would like recognition of my donation to be:
　　■ Individual donation　■ Corporate donation　■ Different individual

_____
PLEASE PRINT NAME OR COMPANY NAME AS YOU WOULD LIKE IT TO APPEAR

PLEASE PRINT　☐ Mr. ☐ Mrs. ☐ Ms.　　MEMBER NUMBER_____

_____
Last Name (Family Name)　　　First　　　Middle Initial

_____
Title

_____
Address

_____
City　　　State/Province　　　Country ZIP/Postal Code

**Please mail this completed form with your contribution to:
The Research Foundation of CFA Institute • P.O. Box 2082
Charlottesville, VA 22902-2082 USA**

**For more on the Research Foundation of CFA Institute, please visit
www.cfainstitute.org/about/foundation/.**

Named Endowments

The Research Foundation of CFA Institute acknowledges with sincere gratitude the generous contributions of the Named Endowment participants listed below.

Gifts of at least US$100,000 qualify donors for membership in the Named Endowment category, which recognizes in perpetuity the commitment toward unbiased, practitioner-oriented, relevant research that these firms and individuals have expressed through their generous support of the Research Foundation of CFA Institute.

For more on upcoming Research Foundation publications and webcasts, please visit www.cfainstitute.org/about/foundation/.

Research Foundation monographs are online at www.cfapubs.org.

Made in the USA
San Bernardino, CA
18 October 2017